DIRECTIVE (EU) 2022/2464 AS REGARDS CORPORATE SUSTAINABILITY REPORTING (CSRD)

European Union Law Series

This series brings together major works in the field of European Union Law. It features a diverse range of publications, including comprehensive handbooks designed to teach European Union Law, treaties for legal practitioners and academics, monographs on specialised topics and some of the best doctoral dissertations from across Europe. Additionally, it includes publications detailing conference proceedings on topical issues, as well as commentaries on major judgments and decisions handed down by the Court of Justice of the European Union.

DIRECTIVE (EU) 2022/2464 AS REGARDS CORPORATE SUSTAINABILITY REPORTING (CSRD)

Texts and Comments

EUROPEAN UNION LAW SERIES

Edited by

Pascal DURAND, CSRD rapporteur in the European Parliament, former MEP and Member of the Paris Bar Association
Abrial GILBERT-D'HALLUIN, former sherpa to the CSRD rapporteur, Political Advisor in the European Parliament

INTERSENTIA

Intersentia
Lefebvre Sarrut Belgium SA
Rue Haute, 139/6
1000 Bruxelles
Belgium
Email: contact@larcier-intersentia.com

Distribution for the UK and
Rest of the World (incl. Eastern Europe)
Ingram Publisher Services UK
1 Deltic Avenue, Rooksley
Milton Keynes MK13 8LD
United Kingdom
Tel: +44 1752 202 301 | Fax: +44 1752 202 331
Email: orders@nbninternational.com

Distribution for France and Other Countries
Interforum Editis
92 avenue de France
75013 Paris
France

Distribution for the USA and Canada
Independent Publishers Group
Order Department
814 North Franklin Street
Chicago, IL 60610
USA
Tel: +1 800 888 4741 (toll free) | Fax: +1 312 337 5985
Email: orders@ipgbook.com

Directive (EU) 2022/2464 as regards Corporate Sustainability Reporting (CSRD).
Texts and Comments.

ISBN 978-1-83970-566-3
D/2024/7849/121
NUR 820

British Library Cataloguing in Publication Data. A catalogue record for this book is available from the British Library

ACKNOWLEDGMENTS

The text upon which the present work is based is the result of several years of work.
I wish to express my gratitude to all those who contributed to the adoption of this text, and especially, for their political and technical support, their patience, and their personal commitment: Olivia Grégoire, Pascal Demurger, and Marc Boissonnet.
Furthermore, at the European Parliament, I would like to thank all the shadow rapporteurs of the CSRD, their advisers, as well as my entire parliamentary team, with a special mention of Juliette Raulet-Descombey and Berthille Simon.
Last but not least, a big thank you to the Groupe Lefebvre Sarrut teams for believing in this project from the outset, and for contributing so willingly to its realisation.

Pascal Durand

European law more than ever requires clarity. I would therefore like to express my gratitude to all those who have provided their technical or moral support to enable this Directive to come to life and to this present publication to blend its complexity into a single, easy-to-read text.

Abrial Gilbert-d'Halluin

FOREWORD

Pascal Durand

Contrary to what some would have us believe, the Corporate Sustainability Reporting Directive (CSRD) was not born out of the perversity of a few technocrats driven by an evil desire to increase the administrative burden on companies and harm their competitiveness, but out of a real political and economic necessity.

I. THE NEED OF A NEW REGULATORY FRAMEWORK

This legislation has in fact become self-evident due to the inadequacies of the 2014 Non-Financial Reporting Directive (known as the NFRD), which preceded it. The relative failure of this first text stemmed from various causes, the main ones being:

- the small number of companies covered by statutory reporting;
- the absence of shared, mandatory norms and standards, and the failure to take account of the specific nature of certain sectors;
- the impossibility for the companies concerned to know precisely the nature and extent of the information to be disclosed as part of their extra-financial obligations;
- the arbitrary and often fragmented nature of the data disseminated;
- the corresponding lack of reliability, control and certification of published information;
- the absence of any relevant penalty for failing to disclose the required extra-financial information or for disseminating false information;
- the inadequate training in extra-financial issues for legal and accounting professionals, both externally and internally;
- the competing existence of different types of international standards and labels; and
- the difficulty of producing a relevant analysis of the sustainability of a company and its value chain.

From a factual point of view, despite or – in reality – because of the coexistence of numerous international voluntary standards, the absence of regulation became a handicap inasmuch as, schematically, it was the managers or certifiers' level of ambition that defined the nature and quality of the information disclosed.

This situation made the analysis of stakeholders and the information communicated to shareholders, NGOs, and customers arbitrary and random. A few virtuous companies provided too much information, while others provided none. As for the most communicative companies, they were often content to publish, sometimes with fanfare and trumpets, what they considered relevant to their image... This legal vacuum undermined the sincerity of the market and the competition, with virtuous companies whose reliable information was verified finding themselves in the same boat as much less scrupulous operators.

II. A EUROPEAN LEGISLATIVE RESPONSIBILITY

This situation, which oscillated between greenwashing and fragmented information, was becoming legally untenable and clearly could not continue. The market needs security and reliable data, especially when external funding – whether private or public – requires closer control and knowledge of the company. A European legislative reform was therefore needed to overcome this state of uncertainty.

Thus, far from a preconceived notion entertained by certain interest representatives who are often opportunely relayed, the CSRD does not constitute a 'new' administrative burden that would unnecessarily burden companies' operations. On the contrary, it can greatly simplify reporting and analysis by harmonising and standardising the data to be published.

It should therefore be seen first and foremost as an opportunity to rationalise information and create a more objective scorecard on the company's sustainability, and as the end of hemiplegic governance based on a false opposition between a 'financial' vision of the company and its 'extra-financial' counterpart.

In this respect, it is important to note the evolution, which is not just semantic, from a so-called 'extra-financial' directive to a 'sustainability' directive.

The notion of sustainability covers concepts and issues that can also have numerous financial effects; thus, it made no sense to pit the two types of reporting against each other. Impact-based materiality is one of the illustrations of this interweaving of risks and opportunities for the company, and the conditions in which it operates.

However, I do not wish to limit myself to defending the technical merits of the CSRD without pointing out that legislation is the result of a more global reflection on what constitutes the general interest and the common good.

If the representatives of private interests are in their legitimate role when they defend those interests, let me remind you that the general interest is rarely, if ever, the sum of private interests.

The job of the European legislator is to defend the general European interest and to take account of changes in society and the planet when deciding to legislate.

The global context has changed considerably in recent years. The 2015 Paris Agreement recognised the need to take effective, concerted action against the increase in greenhouse gas emissions and climate change, and to preserve resources and biodiversity. The United Nations' guiding principles remind us about the need to combat poverty, slavery, forced labour and all forms of discrimination, and to defend human, trade union and indigenous rights. These are not mere objectives among others, the illustration of a romantic idealism or utopia, but a real categorical imperative, that of preserving the future of our civilisation, of our planet, and to do so while respecting our principles and values, that of a democratic market society, committed to the rule of law and humanism.

And it is in the light of this imperative of higher and general interest that this legislation must also be understood. If Corporate Social Responsibility (CSR) and sustainability information is essential, it is also, if not above all, because the company must play its part in achieving these objectives of general interest. On the one hand, for its own sake, to protect itself from external reputational risks and from the risks that its activities may pose to third parties and to the planet; but also, because companies are key to the future, and among the most effective levers for achieving these general-interest objectives. The fact that the continental European space is one of the most determined to seek – and has been for decades – this fair balance and this temperance between the economy, the environment and society is the specificity, the safeguard and the honour of our Union.

Not legislating on sustainability would be a major political mistake for the Union. Europe's economic sovereignty depends on its ability to define its own standards and rules without waiting for them to be imposed from outside, as in the case of financial matters, for example.

Not legislating would mean refusing to anticipate the changes and upheavals of the 21st century, and leaving ourselves open to the vagaries of an uncertain future, in terms of access to resources and investment, for example.

Not legislating would nullify the collective targets set for carbon neutrality by 2050, and render meaningless a large part of the Green Deal, taxonomy and the preservation of biodiversity on land and in the sea.

Not legislating would mean refusing to listen to and take into account a major change in society regarding the intrinsic qualities of the products consumed, their manufacture and origin, and the growing desire, particularly among the younger generations, to make sustainable governance and CSR a priority for their future, and to no longer see a company's profitability alone as the alpha and omega of any industrial, commercial or service activity.

The reality is obviously complex, and not every purchase is dictated by ethical or moral considerations – far from it. On the one hand, a company's reputation can deteriorate very quickly if it is shown to have lied or concealed information about activities that are harmful to the planet, such as active participation in uncontrolled deforestation, attacks on indigenous populations or the use of forced or child labour. On the other hand, it can be extremely advantageous for a company to communicate, under objective and certified control, about the ethical nature of its production, mobility or human-relations choices; the search for meaning is not a dirty word, even in commercial matters.

III. AN OBLIGATION 'TO SAY', NOT 'TO DO'

Legally, the CSRD is not an 'obligation to do', but an 'obligation to say': it is an obligation of transparency incumbent on the company, in the very same way as for the publication of its financial statements and company accounts.

As with its free choice of investments, nothing will force a company to choose a specific transition plan or specific means of reducing its carbon footprint and limiting its emissions; but respecting its choices and its declarations on the applicability of norms and standards to its activities will help it in its governance and in its relations with all its stakeholders.

All these considerations, described earlier as technical and political, led the European Union to vote for the CSRD by a very large majority.

However, legislating in the general interest does not mean ignoring particular interests, or sidelining stakeholders in order to define rules that would quickly be seen as 'out of touch'.

IV. THE CENTRAL ROLE OF EFRAG

To avoid these pitfalls, the European Commission took care to involve business and audit professionals in its deliberations, both upstream and downstream of its proposal. The partnership between the Commission, then the Parliament and the Council, with the European Financial Reporting Advisory Group (EFRAG), to define the European standards and norms (the ESRS), was a guarantee of rigour and realism.

The task was immense but, as mentioned above, EFRAG was not starting from scratch. Numerous sustainability reporting standards already existed, different international standards were competing with each other, and large companies had become accustomed to communicating extra-financial information through the NFRD.

What was needed was 'simply' to give shape to these different standards, rationalise them and align them with the political objectives defined by the Commission and the European co-legislators, around the Green Deal, the Common Agricultural Policy and numerous specific pieces of legislation. We needed to restore coherence to the European internal market, without undermining its competitiveness, and free it from uncertainty, so that investments – particularly 'green' ones – could be made with full knowledge of the facts.

The decision to entrust this work to an independent technical body, previously responsible for drawing up financial norms and standards, was the subject of an initial political discussion in Parliament.

To shed some light on the legislative process, it is important to remember that the European Parliament does not have a stable, permanent political majority, as is the case in many national parliaments. The texts, which are initiated by the Commission alone, are the subject of close negotiations between groups representing 27 nationalities and seven political groups, not counting the non-attached Members... For some groups, it was not self-evident that, as a body with a financial culture, EFRAG should be entrusted with drafting sustainability norms and standards. However, this was the majority decision, for a major pragmatic reason: this group already existed, it functioned perfectly, it was aware of the difficulties encountered with the NFRD, and its competence was not contested. Furthermore, this choice was consistent with placing sustainability norms and standards at the same level of rigour and definition as financial norms, and not pitting one against the other. It was nevertheless decided to ask, in agreement with the EFRAG Board and the Commission, that EFRAG's governance evolve and that a board dedicated to sustainability, including more stakeholders such as certain European NGOs and trade unions, be made permanent.

This point, which was one of the first to be addressed in our legislative debates, illustrates the European culture of compromise. Many more were later negotiated in this text, some agreements being more difficult than others to reach.

V. EXTRATERRITORIALITY

The next issue, which was particularly close to my heart, concerned extraterritoriality. It was painful, not to say unbearable, to observe during all my years as an MEP the naivety or weakness with which the European Union opened its borders to all winds, imposed rules and standards on its own nationals, legal entities and individuals alike, without having the will or the courage to impose compliance with these same norms and standards on players of non-EU nationality in our internal market.

Since the last agricultural crisis, everyone has been familiar with the mirror clauses that the EU wants to impose in its free trade agreements, but in legal or commercial terms, this was generally not even envisaged.

This lack of reciprocity was even more incomprehensible given that the other major international operators, the USA and China, did not hesitate to impose their own rules and conditions to operate in their domestic markets.

I was pleased to note, from our first meetings, that the groups unanimously shared this view and that all of them, without exception, would support a major change to the Commission's proposal: requiring non-EU companies to report in the same way as European companies if they wanted to obtain the right to operate on our internal market. Once this decision had been taken, all that remained was to defend it to an initially extremely reluctant Commission, for practical reasons of feasibility and control. The Council, for its part, agreed without major difficulty.

After tough negotiations with the Commission, a compromise was finally reached, the substance of which you will read in the body of this publication. This principle of extraterritoriality now has the great merit of existing; I am convinced it will create a precedent that will make the internal market fairer for our businesses, and make the Union stronger and more respected in the rest of the world.

VI. EXTENDED SCOPE

The third point that was the subject of heated debate was the scope of the directive, and more specifically its extension to SMEs. While there was no debate about extending the application of the directive beyond the large companies covered by the NFRD, the discussion about the limit of the extension was very open. The Commission proposed a threshold of 250 employees and EUR 40 million turnover, and wanted to be able to extend the CSRD to listed SMEs, while some parties wanted to raise the threshold, and others, to lower it.

On the face of it, this debate might seem relatively straightforward: except for a few cases, SMEs do not have the legal structures, financial or human resources to meet the CSRD's ESRS (European Sustainability Reporting Standards) reporting and certification specifications. However, the devil is often in the details.

Given that large companies subject to the CSRD or the duty of vigilance will be obliged to disseminate information relating to their value and subcontracting chains, most of which are made up of SMEs, the latter will *de facto* be subject to some of these reporting obligations. However, this information will be required and defined by the principal alone, and will be neither regulated by law nor consistent within the same sector. The patchwork of information that was one of the weaknesses of the NFRD will be repeated here. Not defining the norms and standards to be communicated by SMEs is not necessarily a service to them, as it in no way constitutes a guarantee against the complexity or cost of reporting. On the contrary, it opens the door to obligations imposed by principals without any real framework, leading to major disparities in the market, and undermining competition.

Furthermore, not providing sustainability information for SMEs risks cutting off or at least limiting their access to finance. From the moment that investors and credit institutions must account for and provide information on the sustainability of their investments or loans, they will need to analyse the situation of the company concerned. The absence of any sustainability information will then be a formidable obstacle, as investors need reliable information before making their decisions.

These points having been debated, and the desire of certain groups not to extend the scope of the CSRD to SMEs being all the more inflexible as the election period loomed, it was agreed to maintain the exemption, while asking EFRAG to define specific norms and standards for SMEs in order to define the nature and extent of the information that they will have to provide, but on a purely voluntary basis, and to postpone until 2027 the implementation of the Directive for listed SMEs. The advantage of this compromise solution is that it provides a lighter, more flexible and consistent framework for SMEs, while leaving them free to decide whether or not to comply with the reporting requirements. It also has the merit of making it possible, when the text is reviewed, to study the real impact of this voluntary framework and to refine the scope of the CSRD.

Regarding the SME topic, it is necessary to mention the influence, within the European Union, of certain interest groups. When their activities are fair and transparent, the presence of interest representatives in the legislative process is useful, if not indispensable. They know their respective sectors better than anyone else and can provide information on the risks or opportunities of legislative change. But this action becomes highly open to criticism when it is intended to block any progress and takes the form of demagoguery or public caricature to discredit the reform. In this case, certain organisations, either out of self-interest or conservative ideology, tried to oppose an ambitious implementation of the CSRD and discredited it through the press, while also mobilising their networks of political and economic influence.

These propaganda actions are harmful to democracy: journalists and the general public do not necessarily have access to all the information, so simplistic arguments can sometimes bear fruit. Fortunately, the overwhelming majority of the specialist and European press has done a great deal of work in deciphering the facts and has systematically respected the adversarial process to disentangle the true from the false.

VII. TARGETED ATTACKS ON THE TEXT

So, as the text progressed, we were subjected to targeted and concerted attacks claiming that:

- all European companies would be affected indiscriminately by reporting and that their operating and auditing costs would skyrocket because of this new administrative burden;
- European standardisation was totally unnecessary, since international standards, particularly in the field of climate, would be defined and all that was needed was to apply them;
- international standards on human and social rights and the environment were too vague to be applicable; and
- the certification of two reports, one financial, the other sustainability, would lead to blockages and uncertainty within companies.

After they failed to block or delay the implementation of the legislation, since it was eventually adopted and supported by the overwhelming majority of stakeholders, the action of these interest groups then focused on denigrating EFRAG's work on ESRS, indicating that the proposed standards constituted an incomprehensible and technocratic white elephant that would definitively undermine the competitiveness of European companies and the attractiveness of the Union.

More subtly and insidiously, others, without criticising the principle of the CSRD, wanted to considerably reduce its scope by limiting the mandatory norms and standards to climate issues alone, thus postponing indefinitely the publication of information on social and human rights, and biodiversity.

The argument most often heard, that would reappear later during the European election campaign, was the alleged administrative overload caused by European legislation and its overly technical nature.

Indeed, some politicians have used one of the mantras of the von der Leyen Commission to bolster their arguments, that of 'better' regulation, which has gradually been transformed into 'less' regulation, paving the way for the demagogues of simplistic and essentially cosmetic deregulation.

As far as norms and standards are concerned, these external interventions have finally borne fruit, albeit to a limited extent, since some standards have been postponed while others have been reduced and some, such as the disclosure of biodiversity transition plans, have seen their mandatory nature removed.

However, the essential elements have been preserved, and are included in the final text and in the ESRSs already published or to be published for certain specific sectors from June 2026.

VIII. COMPROMISE

In order to meet expectations and maintain a large majority in Parliament and the Council while retaining almost all of the Commission's proposal, we have tried to take account of the various constructive criticisms and to ward off attempts to block the process.

We have reiterated the need to develop specifically European legislation, particularly regarding double materiality, while ensuring that the climate aspect of this legislation is compatible and interoperable with future international standards. This express intention to establish equivalence will mean that transnational companies will exempt them from declaring several types of information for different geographical sectors.

We have also taken care to list, in the recitals, the various reference texts on social and environmental matters so that operators, inspectors, certifiers and, where appropriate, administrative and judicial bodies can have certain and reliable sources and a legal basis for reporting obligations. These texts will also be of great help when it comes to examining compliance with obligations of due diligence, for example.

The issue of control and certification also occupied us for a long time. While the principle of having a certified sustainability report was self-evident, integrating and merging it with the financial report was not. Nor was it considered appropriate to entrust the same certifying body with the audit and subsequent drafting of both reports. The risk of sustainability issues being taken over by financial experts was not negligible, and the temptation to arbitrate in favour of financial imperatives and criteria is not a mere figment of the imagination. However, no majority, neither in the Parliament, nor in the Commission and even less in the Council, could be found to dissociate the audit and control of sustainability, the argument most often used being that of the alleged increase in costs.

This argument is a perfect illustration of the aforementioned difficulty of an objective and rational debate on technical subjects. Yet it is easy to see that a handful of audit firms in the EU have a virtual monopoly on financial reporting – the famous Big Four, not to name them specifically– and are keen to extend their activities to sustainability issues. Supported in this hegemonic desire by a large proportion of EU Member States, intense lobbying – to put it mildly – has been undertaken in an attempt to limit the possibility of using independent third parties for sustainability certification and to prohibit double auditing.

A quick word about the alleged increase in costs that would result from dual auditing or the appointment of an independent sustainability certifier: while the first reports have not yet been finalised, requests from financial auditors for fees relating to sustainability do not show any significant reduction compared with those of an external expert.

Regarding the nature of reporting obligations, certification and control, we have chosen to remain moderate, with limited assurance initially, then reasonable assurance thereafter. It was not a question, particularly for medium-sized companies and auditors, of going from 'nothing to everything'. When the Directive is revised, the Commission will also examine any need to strengthen its application.

IX. MAKE IT A REALITY

The implementation of the CSRD now depends on the will of the stakeholders to make it a reality, and a useful and effective tool in our new economy. It also requires the unwavering commitment of the Member States, which retain a monopoly on the organisation of auditing, certification and sanctions for any non- or false declarations.

However, it is in the commitment of the Member States that the greatest uncertainty lies, because without political will and courage, it is rare for a legal text to be fully effective. They now have the opportunity to strengthen the power of independent control bodies dedicated to sustainability, and to make sustainability the right counterpart to mere financial logic.

This book, which aims to be educational and exhaustive, offers all the stakeholders a pragmatic and efficient CSRD perspective. The role of the legislator ends here; that of the players in this new economy of the 21st century, begins.

Pascal Durand

METHODOLOGY

This book presents the European Directive (EU) 2022/2464, known as the Corporate Sustainability Reporting Directive (CSRD). It aims to enhance comprehension by contextualising, elucidating, and commenting on the directive, article by article.

The CSRD is an amending legal act that introduces new rules concerning sustainability reporting, modifying over fifty legal articles within four major legislative texts of the European Union:

- Directive 2013/34/EU, known as the Accounting Directive;
- Directive 2004/109/EC, known as the Transparency Directive;
- Directive 2006/43/EC, known as the Audit Directive; and
- Regulation (EU) 537/2014, known as the Audit Regulation.

To properly understand and implement the EU law applicable to sustainability reporting, it is essential to refer to these four major texts as amended by the CSRD. However, these texts include numerous provisions unrelated to sustainability reporting. For the sake of readability and efficiency, this book compiles all the relevant articles or extracts from these four texts that pertain exclusively to sustainability reporting.

The initial phase of this work involved the following steps, starting from the text of the CSRD itself:

- reproducing the structure of the directive;
- integrating the amended articles from the four aforementioned texts (Parts I to IV of this book); and
- including articles specific to the implementation of the CSRD (presented in Part V of this book).

To ensure a thorough understanding and correct application of the CSRD, this book goes beyond mere reproduction of the directive's text:

- When the CSRD amends a single paragraph of an article in the Accounting Directive, for example, we have chosen to reproduce a more comprehensive extract or the entire article, thus providing its consolidated version.
- To ensure the accessibility of each provision, if an article referenced is not present in the table of contents, its title or summary is indicated in a footnote.
- Additional texts not amended by the CSRD, such as the Taxonomy Regulation, which are crucial for implementing the CSRD, have also been added.

- Furthermore, this book provides commentary – or Recitals of the CSRD – on essential articles of law that have been amended, newly introduced, or are specific to the CSRD.

This work constitutes a comprehensive compilation of all EU legal rules necessary for implementing the CSRD. It is designed to help navigate the various legal texts related to sustainability reporting or intrinsically linked to it, thereby facilitating the application of this complex body of law.

We hope this compilation will be a valuable resource for you.

TYPOGRAPHY USED

The text of the CSRD directive is reproduced using simple typography.

- Example: 'The coordination measures prescribed by Articles 19a [...]'

  The additions necessary for the consolidations (Example A) and/or contextualisation of the directive (copy and paste of a mentioned Article) have been put in square brackets. Summaries of a legal provision (Example B) and titles (Example C) of the Articles not present in the table of contents have been put in footnotes.

- Example A:

  '[1. The power to adopt delegated acts is conferred on the Commission subject to the conditions laid down in this Article.]

  2. The power to adopt delegated acts referred to in Article 1(2), Article 3(13), Articles 29b, 29c and 40b, and Article 46(2) shall be conferred on the Commission for a period of 5 years from 5 January 2023. The Commission shall draw up a report in respect of the delegation of power not later than nine months before the end of the 5-year period. The delegation of power shall be tacitly extended for periods of an identical duration, unless the European Parliament or the Council opposes such extension not later than three months before the end of each period.'

- Example B:

  '1. Large undertakings, and small and medium-sized undertakings, except micro undertakings, which are public-interest entities as defined in point (a) of point (1) of Article 2[1] shall include in the management report information necessary to understand the undertaking's impacts on sustainability matters, and information necessary to understand how sustainability matters affect the undertaking's development, performance and position.'

  [1] Listed companies on regulated markets of EU Member States.

- Example C:

  'In the context of point (ii) of the first subparagraph, the Commission shall also adopt, by means of delegated acts in accordance with Article 27(2a), (2b) and (2c), and subject to the conditions of Articles 27a[1] and 27b[2], measures concerning the assessment of standards relevant to the issuers of more than one country.'

  [1] 'Revocation of the delegation'.
  [2] 'Objections to delegated acts'.

TABLE OF CONTENTS

PART III
AMENDMENTS TO DIRECTIVE 2006/43/EC

PART IV
AMENDMENTS TO REGULATION (EU) 537/2014

PART V
TRANSPOSITION AND IMPLEMENTATION OF DIRECTIVE (EU) 2022/2464

PART I

Amendments to Directive 2013/34/EU

ARTICLE 1
SCOPE

Extract

[...]

3. The coordination measures prescribed by Articles 19a, 29a, 29d, 30 and 33, point (aa) of the second subparagraph of Article 34(1),[1] Article 34(2)[2] and (3)[3] and Article 51[4] of this Directive shall also apply to the laws, regulations and administrative provisions of the Member States relating to the following undertakings regardless of their legal form, provided that those undertakings are large undertakings, or small and medium-sized undertakings, except micro undertakings, which are public-interest entities as defined in point (a) of point (1) of Article 2 of this Directive:
   (a) insurance undertakings within the meaning of Article 2(1) of Council Directive 91/674/EEC of 19 December 1991;[5]
   (b) credit institutions as defined in point (1) of Article 4(1) of Regulation (EU) No 575/2013 of the European Parliament and of the Council of 26 June 2013.[6]

   Member States may choose not to apply the coordination measures referred to in the first subparagraph of this paragraph to the undertakings listed in

---

1 It introduces a general requirement of audit for public-interest entities, medium-sized and large undertakings.

2 It prescribes an application mutatis mutandis of the requirement for undertaking's financial statements and management reports to consolidated financial statements and management reports.

3 It sets the possibility for Member States to allow a statutory auditor or an audit firm other than the ones carrying out the statutory audit of financial statements to express an assurance opinion on the sustainability statement.

4 'Penalties', Member States shall provide for penalties applicable to infringements of the national provisions adopted in accordance with the Accounting Directive. The penalties provided for shall be effective, proportionate and dissuasive.

5 An 'insurance undertaking' means a direct life or non-life insurance undertaking which has received authorization in an EU Member State.

6 A 'credit institution' refers to entities primarily engaged in accepting deposits or other repayable funds from the public, provided that such activity involves the operation of payment accounts.

points (2) to (23) of Article 2(5) of Directive 2013/36/EU of the European Parliament and of the Council of 26 June 2013.[7]

4. The coordination measures prescribed by Articles 19a, 29a and 29d, shall not apply to financial products listed in points (b)[8] and (f)[9] of point (12) of Article 2 of Regulation (EU) 2019/2088 of the European Parliament and of the Council of 27 November 2019.
5. The coordination measures prescribed by Articles 40a to 40d shall also apply to the laws, regulations and administrative provisions of the Member States relating to subsidiary undertakings and branches of undertakings which are not governed by the law of a Member State but whose legal form is comparable with the types of undertakings listed in Annex I.[10]

I. ADDITIONAL TEXTS

A. ADDITIONAL TEXT NO. 1

Directive 2013/36/EU of the European Parliament and of the Council of 26 June 2013, Capital Requirements Directive (CRD), Article 2(5), points (2) to (23)

[...]

(2) central banks;

(3) post office giro institutions;

(4) in Denmark, the 'Eksport Kredit Fonden', the 'Eksport Kredit Fonden A/S', the 'Danmarks Skibskredit A/S' and the 'KommuneKredit';

(5) in Germany, the 'Kreditanstalt für Wiederaufbau', 'Landwirtschaftliche Rentenbank', 'Bremer Aufbau-Bank GmbH', 'Hamburgische Investitions- und Förderbank', 'Investitionsbank Berlin', 'Investitionsbank des Landes Brandenburg', 'Investitionsbank Schleswig-Holstein', 'Investitions- und Förderbank Niedersachsen – NBank', 'Investitions- und Strukturbank Rheinland-Pfalz', 'Landeskreditbank Baden-Württemberg – Förderbank', 'LfA Förderbank Bayern', 'NRW.BANK', 'Saarländische Investitionskreditbank AG', 'Sächsische Aufbaubank – Förderbank', 'Thüringer Aufbaubank', undertakings which are recognised under the 'Wohnungsgemeinnützigkeitsgesetz' as bodies of State housing policy and are not mainly engaged in banking transactions, and undertakings recognised under that law as non-profit housing undertakings;

7 See additional text No. 1, p. 4.
8 An alternative investment fund (AIF).
9 An Undertakings for Collective Investments in Transferable Securities (UCITS).
10 See additional text No. 2, p. 5.

(6) in Estonia, the 'hoiu-laenuühistud', as cooperative undertakings that are recognised under the 'hoiu-laenuühistu seadus';
(7) in Ireland, the Strategic Banking Corporation of Ireland, credit unions and friendly societies;
(8) in Greece, the 'Ταμείο Παρακαταθηκών και Δανείων' (Tamio Parakatathikon kai Danion);
(9) in Spain, the 'Instituto de Crédito Oficial';
(10) in France, the 'Caisse des dépôts et consignations';
(11) in Croatia, the 'kreditne unije' and the 'Hrvatska banka za obnovu i razvitak';
(12) in Italy, the 'Cassa depositi e prestiti';
(13) in Latvia, the 'krājaizdevu sabiedrības', undertakings that are recognised under the 'krājaizdevu sabiedrību likums' as cooperative undertakings rendering financial services solely to their members;
(14) in Lithuania, the 'kredito unijos' other than the 'centrinės kredito unijos';
(15) in Hungary, the 'MFB Magyar Fejlesztési Bank Zártkörűen Működő Részvénytársaság' and the 'Magyar Export-Import Bank Zártkörűen Működő Részvénytársaság';
(16) in Malta, 'The Malta Development Bank';
(17) in the Netherlands, the 'Nederlandse Investeringsbank voor Ontwikkelingslanden NV', the 'NV Noordelijke Ontwikkelingsmaatschappij', the 'NV Limburgs Instituut voor Ontwikkeling en Financiering', the 'Ontwikkelingsmaatschappij Oost-Nederland NV' and kredietunies;
(18) in Austria, undertakings recognised as housing associations in the public interest and the 'Österreichische Kontrollbank AG';
(19) in Poland, the 'Spółdzielcze Kasy Oszczędnościowo — Kredytowe' and the 'Bank Gospodarstwa Krajowego';
(20) in Portugal, the 'Caixas Económicas' existing on 1 January 1986 with the exception of those incorporated as limited companies and of the 'Caixa Económica Montepio Geral';
(21) in Slovenia, the 'SID-Slovenska izvozna in razvojna banka, d.d. Ljubljana';
(22) in Finland, the 'Teollisen yhteistyön rahasto Oy/Fonden för industriellt samarbete AB', and the 'Finnvera Oyj/Finnvera Abp';
(23) in Sweden, the 'Svenska Skeppshypotekskassan';

B. ADDITIONAL TEXT NO. 2

Directive 2013/34/EU of the European Parliament and of the Council of 26 June 2013, Accounting Directive, Annex I

TYPES OF UNDERTAKING REFERRED TO IN POINT (A) OF ARTICLE 1(1)

- Belgium:
  la société anonyme/de naamloze vennootschap, la société en commandite par actions/de commanditaire vennootschap op aandelen, la société privée à responsabilité limitée/de besloten vennootschap met beperkte aansprakelijkheid, la société coopérative à responsabilité limitée/de coöperatieve vennootschap met beperkte aansprakelijkheid;
- Bulgaria:
  акционерно дружество, дружество с ограничена отговорност, командитно дружество с акции;
- the Czech Republic:
  společnost s ručením omezeným, akciová společnost;
- Denmark:
  aktieselskaber, kommanditaktieselskaber, anpartsselskaber;
- Germany:
  die Aktiengesellschaft, die Kommanditgesellschaft auf Aktien, die Gesellschaft mit beschränkter Haftung;
- Estonia:
  aktsiaselts, osaühing;
- Ireland:
  public companies limited by shares or by guarantee, private companies limited by shares or by guarantee;
- Greece:
  η ανώνυμη εταιρία, η εταιρία περιορισμένης ευθύνης, η ετερόρρυθμη κατά μετοχές εταιρία;
- Spain:
  la sociedad anónima, la sociedad comanditaria por acciones, la sociedad de responsabilidad limitada;
- France:
  la société anonyme, la société en commandite par actions, la société à responsabilité limitée, la société par actions simplifiée;
- In Croatia:
  dioničko društvo, društvo s ograničenom odgovornošću;
- Italy:
  la società per azioni, la società in accomandita per azioni, la società a responsabilità limitata;
- Cyprus:
  Δημόσιες εταιρείες περιορισμένης ευθύνης με μετοχές ή με εγγύηση, ιδιωτικές εταιρείες περιορισμένης ευθύνης με μετοχές ή με εγγύηση;
- Latvia:
  akciju sabiedrība, sabiedrība ar ierobežotu atbildību;
- Lithuania:
  akcinės bendrovės, uždarosios akcinės bendrovės;
- Luxembourg:

la société anonyme, la société en commandite par actions, la société à responsabilité limitée;
- Hungary:
részvénytársaság, korlátolt felelősségű társaság;
- Malta:
kumpanija pubblika —public limited liability company, kumpannija privata —private limited liability company,
soċjeta in akkomandita bil-kapital maqsum f'azzjonijiet —partnership en commandite with the capital divided into shares;
- the Netherlands:
de naamloze vennootschap, de besloten vennootschap met beperkte aansprakelijkheid;
- Austria:
die Aktiengesellschaft, die Gesellschaft mit beschränkter Haftung;
- Poland:
spółka akcyjna, spółka z ograniczoną odpowiedzialnością, spółka komandytowo-akcyjna;
- Portugal:
a sociedade anónima, de responsabilidade limitada, a sociedade em comandita por ações, a sociedade por quotas de responsabilidade limitada;
- Romania:
societate pe acţiuni, societate cu răspundere limitată, societate în comandită pe acţiuni.
- Slovenia:
delniška družba, družba z omejeno odgovornostjo, komanditna delniška družba;
- Slovakia:
akciová spoločnosť, spoločnosť s ručením obmedzeným;
- Finland:
yksityinen osakeyhtiö/privat aktiebolag, julkinen osakeyhtiö/publikt aktiebolag;
- Sweden:
aktiebolag;
- the United Kingdom:
public companies limited by shares or by guarantee, private companies limited by shares or by guarantee

ARTICLE 2
DEFINITIONS

Extract

[(1) 'public-interest entities' means undertakings within the scope of Article 1 which are:

(a) governed by the law of a Member State and whose transferable securities are admitted to trading on a regulated market of any Member State within the meaning of point (14) of Article 4(1) of Directive 2004/39/EC of the European Parliament and of the Council of 21 April 2004 on markets in financial instruments;

(b) credit institutions as defined in point (1) of Article 4 of Directive 2006/48/EC of the European Parliament and of the Council of 14 June 2006 relating to the taking up and pursuit of the business of credit institutions, other than those referred to in Article 2 of that Directive;

(c) insurance undertakings within the meaning of Article 2(1) of Council Directive 91/674/EEC of 19 December 1991 on the annual accounts of insurance undertakings; or

(d) designated by Member States as public-interest entities, for instance undertakings that are of significant public relevance because of the nature of their business, their size or the number of their employees;]

[...]

(5) 'net turnover' means the amounts derived from the sale of products and the provision of services after deducting sales rebates and value added tax and other taxes directly linked to turnover; however, for insurance undertakings referred to in point (a) of the first subparagraph of Article 1(3) of this Directive, 'net turnover' shall be defined in accordance with Article 35 and point 2 of Article 66 of Council Directive 91/674/EEC of 19 December 1991;[11] for credit institutions referred to in point (b) of the first subparagraph of Article 1(3) of this Directive, 'net turnover' shall be defined in accordance with point (c) of Article 43(2) of Council Directive

[11] See additional texts Nos. 3–4, pp. 10–11.

86/635/EEC of 8 December 1991;[12] and for undertakings falling under the scope of Article 40a(1) of this Directive, 'net turnover' means the revenue as defined by or within the meaning of the financial reporting framework on the basis of which the financial statements of the undertaking are prepared;

[...]

(17) 'sustainability matters' means environmental, social and human rights, and governance factors, including sustainability factors defined in point (24) of Article 2 of Regulation (EU) 2019/2088;[13]
(18) 'sustainability reporting' means reporting information related to sustainability matters in accordance with Articles 19a, 29a and 29d;
(19) 'key intangible resources' means resources without physical substance on which the business model of the undertaking fundamentally depends and which are a source of value creation for the undertaking;
(20) 'independent assurance services provider' means a conformity assessment body accredited in accordance with Regulation (EC) No 765/2008 of the European Parliament and of the Council of July 2008 for the specific conformity assessment activity referred to in point (aa) of the second subparagraph of Article 34(1) of this Directive.

I. ADDITIONAL TEXTS

A. ADDITIONAL TEXT NO. 3

Directive 91/674/EEC of the Council of 19 December 1991,
Annual accounts and consolidated accounts of insurance undertakings,
Article 35

Non-life-insurance technical account: item I (1) (a)
Life-assurance technical account: item II (1) (a)
Gross premiums written

Gross premiums written shall comprise all amounts due during the financial year in respect of insurance contracts regardless of the fact that such amounts may relate in whole or in part to a later financial year, and shall include inter alia:

(i) premiums yet to be written, where the premium calculation can be done only at the end of the year:

---

12 See additional text No. 5, p. 11.

13 'Sustainability factors' means environmental, social and employee matters, respect for human rights, anti-corruption and anti-bribery matters.

(ii) • single premiums, including annuity premiums,
- in life assurance, single premiums resulting from bonus and rebate provisions in so far as they must be considered as premiums on the basis of contracts and where national legislation requires or permits their being shown under premiums;

(iii) additional premiums in the case of half-yearly, quarterly or monthly payments and additional payments from policyholders for expenses borne by the insurance undertaking;

(iv) in the case of co-insurance, the undertaking's portion of total premiums;

(v) reinsurance premiums due from ceding and retroceding insurance undertakings, including portfolio entries, after deduction of:
- portfolio withdrawals credited to ceding and retroceding insurance undertakings, and
- cancellations.

The above amounts shall not include the amounts of taxes or charges levied with premiums.

B. ADDITIONAL TEXT NO. 4

Directive 91/674/EEC of the Council of 19 December 1991,
Annual accounts and consolidated accounts of insurance undertakings,
Article 66, point 2

2. the information referred to in the first and second indents of Article 9(2), namely:
   - the amount of the fixed assets, and
   - the net turnover,

shall be replaced by particulars of the gross premiums written as defined in Article 35 of this Directive;

C. ADDITIONAL TEXT NO. 5

Directive 86/635/EEC of the Council of 8 December 1986,
Annual accounts and consolidated accounts of banks
and other financial institutions, Article 43(2)(c)

(c) The information referred to in the first two indents of Article 9 (2) of Directive 83/349/EEC, namely:
- the amount of the fixed assets and
- the net turnover

shall be replaced by:

- the sum of items 1, 3, 4, 6 and 7 in Article 27 or B 1, B 2, B 3, B 4 and B 7 in Article 28 of this Directive.

II. COMMENTS

A. FIRST COMMENT

What are Sustainability Matters?

Sustainability matters are environmental, social, economic and employee matters, respect for human rights, anti-corruption and anti-bribery matters, as well as other specific entities' governance matters. These topics are more precisely defined in the European Sustainability Reporting Standards (ESRS) – e.g. diversity policies or child labour when it comes to governance and human rights respectively, and should be consistent with the list of the Sustainability-related disclosures in the financial services sector Regulation (SFDR).

B. SECOND COMMENT

What is an 'Independent Assurance Services Provider'?

'Independent assurance services providers' (IASPs) are firms other than the usual auditors of financial information that are allowed by Member States to audit sustainability information. Depending on the local legal frameworks, IASPs can be either sustainability specialists, lawyers, or any other entity accredited to provide sustainability assurance.

Statutory auditors or audit firms are required to express an opinion based on a limited assurance engagement on the compliance of the sustainability reporting based on the ESRS, on the process carried out by the undertaking to identify the information that is material and whether this information has been properly marked-up electronically in compliance with the European Single Electronic Format (ESEF).[14] The same goes for IASPs.

Regulation (EC) No 765/2008, which sets out the requirements for accreditation, mandates that accreditation bodies such as 'independent assurance services providers' must meet specific criteria and be officially recognised by competent authorities within the European Union. These authorities are responsible for assessing the competence and reliability of conformity assessment

[14] See comment p. 77.

bodies, such as testing laboratories and certification bodies, or ensuring they adhere to relevant standards and regulations. The regulation establishes a framework for the accreditation process, including transparency requirements, impartiality, and competence assessments, to promote consistency and trust in conformity assessment activities across the EU.

C. THIRD COMMENT

Accounting Rules for Banks and Other Financial Institutions within the European Union

The provision of Article 43(2) of 86/635/EEC mandates banks and financial institutions to disclose detailed information in their financial statements.

- Some rules don't apply: Certain rules from Directive 83/349/EEC (this Directive has been repealed by Directive 2013/34/EU) don't apply to banks. These articles cover general rules for preparing consolidated accounts, but banks have specific accounting needs.
- Special conditions for exemption: If a bank doesn't have to prepare consolidated accounts, some conditions might apply:
  - the parent bank must guarantee the debts of the subsidiary, and this guarantee must be shown in the subsidiary's financial statements;
  - the parent company must be a bank or credit institutions.
- Different reporting for fixed assets and turnover: Instead of using the usual terms for reporting fixed assets and turnover, banks must use specific financial items from their own balance sheet, as outlined in Articles 27 and 28 of the Directive 86/635/EEC.
- Exclusion of certain subsidiaries: If a bank temporarily owns another bank (for rescue or reorganisation), this subsidiary might not be included in the consolidated accounts. However, the subsidiary's annual accounts must be attached, and additional details about the rescue operation need to be explained in the notes.
- Unified management of banks: Under certain circumstancies, Member States can allow the consolidation of banks that aren't legally connected (like a parent-subsidiary relationship) but are managed together as if they were one entity.

ARTICLE 19
CONTENTS OF THE MANAGEMENT REPORT

[1. The management report shall include a fair review of the development and performance of the undertaking's business and of its position, together with a description of the principal risks and uncertainties that it faces. The review shall be a balanced and comprehensive analysis of the development and performance of the undertaking's business and of its position, consistent with the size and complexity of the business. To the extent necessary for an understanding of the undertaking's development, performance or position, the analysis shall include both financial and, where appropriate, non-financial key performance indicators relevant to the particular business, including information relating to environmental and employee matters. In providing the analysis, the management report shall, where appropriate, include references to, and additional explanations of, amounts reported in the annual financial statements.]

Large undertakings, and small and medium-sized undertakings, except micro undertakings, which are public-interest entities as defined in point (a) of point (1) of Article 2[15] shall report information on the key intangible resources and explain how the business model of the undertaking fundamentally depends on such resources and how such resources are a source of value creation for the undertaking.

[2. The management report shall also give an indication of:

a) the undertaking's likely future development;
b) activities in the field of research and development;
c) the information concerning acquisitions of own shares prescribed by Article 24(2) of Directive 2012/30/EU;[16]
d) the existence of branches of the undertaking; and
e) in relation to the undertaking's use of financial instruments and where material for the assessment of its assets, liabilities, financial position and profit or loss:

---

15 Listed companies on regulated markets of EU Member States.

16 See additional text No. 6, p. 16.

i. the undertaking's financial risk management objectives and policies, including its policy for hedging each major type of forecasted transaction for which hedge accounting is used; and
ii. the undertaking's exposure to price risk, credit risk, liquidity risk and cash flow risk.

3. Member States may exempt small undertakings from the obligation to prepare management reports, provided that they require the information referred to in Article 24(2) of Directive 2012/30/EU concerning the acquisition by an undertaking of its own shares to be given in the notes to the financial statements.
4. Member States may exempt small and medium-sized undertakings from the obligation set out in the third subparagraph of paragraph 1 in so far as it relates to non-financial information].

I. ADDITIONAL TEXTS

ADDITIONAL TEXT NO. 6

Directive 2012/30/EU of the European Parliament and the Council of 25 October 2012, Public limited liability companies directive, Article 24(2) (no longer in force)

2. Where the laws of a Member State permit a company to acquire its own shares, either itself or through a person acting in his own name but on the company's behalf, they shall require the annual report to state at least:
   (a) the reasons for acquisitions made during the financial year;
   (b) the number and nominal value or, in the absence of a nominal value, the accountable par of the shares acquired and disposed of during the financial year and the proportion of the subscribed capital which they represent;
   (c) in the case of acquisition or disposal for a value, the consideration for the shares;
   (d) the number and nominal value or, in the absence of a nominal value, the accountable par of all the shares acquired and held by the company and the proportion of the subscribed capital which they represent.

II. COMMENTS

CONTENTS OF THE MANAGEMENT REPORT

A management report is a document prepared annually by the managers of a company that provides a comprehensive overview of the company's business performance, operations, risks, and future prospects. It includes both financial and, where appropriate, non-financial key performance indicators to give stakeholders a clear picture of the company's overall health and strategic direction.

With the introduction of the Corporate Sustainability Reporting Directive (CSRD), Article 19 and Article 19a of Directive 2013/34/EU now requires that companies include detailed sustainability information directly within the management report on top of financial information. This includes information on environmental, social, and governance factors, reflecting the company's impact on and management of sustainability issues.

ARTICLE 19A
SUSTAINABILITY REPORTING

1. Large undertakings, and small and medium-sized undertakings, except micro undertakings, which are public-interest entities as defined in point (a) of point (1) of Article 2[17] shall include in the management report information necessary to understand the undertaking's impacts on sustainability matters,[18] and information necessary to understand how sustainability matters affect the undertaking's development, performance and position.
   The information referred to in the first subparagraph shall be clearly identifiable within the management report, through a dedicated section of the management report.
2. The information referred to in paragraph 1 shall contain:
   a) a brief description of the undertaking's business model and strategy, including:
      i. the resilience of the undertaking's business model and strategy in relation to risks related to sustainability matters;
      ii. the opportunities for the undertaking related to sustainability matters;
      iii. the plans of the undertaking, including implementing actions and related financial and investment plans, to ensure that its business model and strategy are compatible with the transition to a sustainable economy and with the limiting of global warming to 1,5 °C in line with the Paris Agreement under the United Nations Framework Convention on Climate Change adopted on 12 December 2015 (the 'Paris Agreement') and the objective of achieving climate neutrality by 2050 as established in Regulation (EU) 2021/1119 of 30 June 2021,[19] and, where relevant, the exposure of the undertaking to coal-, oil- and gas-related activities;

---

17 Listed companies on regulated markets of EU Member States.

18 Environmental, social and employee matters, respect for human rights, anti-corruption and anti-bribery matters as well as other specific entities' governance matters. These are more precisely defined in accordance with the European Sustainability Reporting Standards (ESRS) (see additional text No. 15, p. 58). For example, it can be diversity policies or child labour when it comes to governance and human rights respectively.

19 'Climate neutrality Regulation' or 'European Climate law'; see additional text No. 7, p. 25.

iv. how the undertaking's business model and strategy take account of the interests of the undertaking's stakeholders and of the impacts of the undertaking on sustainability matters;
v. how the undertaking's strategy has been implemented with regard to sustainability matters;

b) a description of the time-bound targets related to sustainability matters set by the undertaking, including, where appropriate, absolute greenhouse gas emission reduction targets at least for 2030 and 2050, a description of the progress the undertaking has made towards achieving those targets, and a statement of whether the undertaking's targets related to environmental factors are based on conclusive scientific evidence;
c) a description of the role of the administrative, management and supervisory bodies with regard to sustainability matters, and of their expertise and skills in relation to fulfilling that role or the access such bodies have to such expertise and skills;
d) a description of the undertaking's policies in relation to sustainability matters;
e) information about the existence of incentive schemes linked to sustainability matters which are offered to members of the administrative, management and supervisory bodies;
f) a description of:
i. the due diligence process implemented by the undertaking with regard to sustainability matters, and, where applicable, in line with Union requirements on undertakings to conduct a due diligence process;
ii. the principal actual or potential adverse impacts connected with the undertaking's own operations and with its value chain, including its products and services, its business relationships and its supply chain, actions taken to identify and monitor those impacts, and other adverse impacts which the undertaking is required to identify pursuant to other Union requirements on undertakings to conduct a due diligence process;
iii. any actions taken by the undertaking to prevent, mitigate, remediate or bring an end to actual or potential adverse impacts, and the result of such actions;
g) a description of the principal risks to the undertaking related to sustainability matters, including a description of the undertaking's principal dependencies on those matters, and how the undertaking manages those risks;
h) indicators relevant to the disclosures referred to in points (a) to (g).

Undertakings shall report the process carried out to identify the information that they have included in the management report in accordance with paragraph 1 of this Article. The information listed in the first subparagraph of this paragraph shall include information related to short-, medium- and long-term time horizons, as applicable.

3. Where applicable, the information referred to in paragraphs 1 and 2 shall contain information about the undertaking's own operations and about its value chain, including its products and services, its business relationships and its supply chain.
   For the first three years of the application of the measures to be adopted by the Member States in accordance with Article 5(2) of Directive (EU) 2022/2464 of 16 December 2022, and in the event that not all the necessary information regarding its value chain is available, the undertaking shall explain the efforts made to obtain the necessary information about its value chain, the reasons why not all of the necessary information could be obtained, and its plans to obtain the necessary information in the future.
   Where applicable, the information referred to in paragraphs 1 and 2 shall also contain references to, and additional explanations of, the other information included in the management report in accordance with Article 19, and the amounts reported in the annual financial statements.
   Member States may allow information relating to impending developments or matters in the course of negotiation to be omitted in exceptional cases where, in the duly justified opinion of the members of the administrative, management and supervisory bodies, acting within the competences assigned to them by national law and having collective responsibility for that opinion, the disclosure of such information would be seriously prejudicial to the commercial position of the undertaking, provided that such omission does not prevent a fair and balanced understanding of the undertaking's development, performance and position, and the impact of its activity.
4. Undertakings shall report the information referred to in paragraphs 1 to 3 of this Article in accordance with the sustainability reporting standards adopted pursuant to Article 29b.
5. The management of the undertaking shall inform the workers' representatives at the appropriate level and discuss with them the relevant information and the means of obtaining and verifying sustainability information. The workers' representatives' opinion shall be communicated, where applicable, to the relevant administrative, management or supervisory bodies.
6. By way of derogation from paragraphs 2 to 4 of this Article, and without prejudice to paragraphs 9 and 10 of this Article, small and medium-sized undertakings referred to in paragraph 1 of this Article, small and non-complex institutions defined in point (145) of Article 4(1) of Regulation (EU) No 575/2013 of 26 June 2013,[20] captive insurance undertakings defined in point (2) of Article 13 of Directive 2009/138/EC of 25 November 2009

[20] See additional text No. 8, p. 25.

and captive reinsurance undertakings defined in point (5) of Article 13[21] of that Directive may limit their sustainability reporting to the following information:

a) a brief description of the undertaking's business model and strategy;

b) a description of the undertaking's policies in relation to sustainability matters;

c) the principal actual or potential adverse impacts of the undertaking on sustainability matters, and any actions taken to identify, monitor, prevent, mitigate or remediate such actual or potential adverse impacts;

d) the principal risks to the undertaking related to sustainability matters and how the undertaking manages those risks;

e) key indicators necessary for the disclosures referred to in points (a) to (d).

Small and medium-sized undertakings, small and non-complex institutions and captive insurance and reinsurance undertakings that rely on the derogation referred to in the first subparagraph shall report in accordance with the sustainability reporting standards for small and medium-sized undertakings referred to in Article 29c.

7. For financial years starting before 1 January 2028, by way of derogation from paragraph 1 of this Article, small and medium-sized undertakings which are public-interest entities as defined in point (a) of point (1) of Article 2 may decide not to include in their management report the information referred to in paragraph 1 of this Article. In such cases, the undertaking shall, nevertheless, briefly state in its management report why the sustainability reporting was not provided.
8. Undertakings that comply with the requirements set out in paragraphs 1 to 4 of this Article and undertakings that rely on the derogation laid down in paragraph 6 of this Article shall be deemed to have complied with the requirement set out in the third subparagraph of Article 19(1).
9. Provided that the conditions set out in the second subparagraph of this paragraph are met, an undertaking which is a subsidiary undertaking shall be exempted from the obligations set out in paragraphs 1 to 4 of this Article ('the exempted subsidiary undertaking') if such undertaking and its subsidiary undertakings are included in the consolidated management report of a parent undertaking, drawn up in accordance with Articles 29[22] and 29a. An undertaking which is a subsidiary undertaking of a parent undertaking that is established in a third country shall also be exempted from the obligations set out in paragraphs 1 to 4 of this Article where such undertaking and its subsidiary undertakings are included in the consolidated sustainability reporting of that parent undertaking that is established in a

[21] See additional text No. 9, p. 26.

[22] 'Consolidated management reporting'; see additional text No. 10, p. 27.

third country and where that consolidated sustainability reporting is carried out in accordance with the sustainability reporting standards adopted pursuant to Article 29b or in a manner equivalent to those sustainability reporting standards, as determined in accordance with an implementing act on the equivalence of sustainability reporting standards adopted pursuant to the third subparagraph of Article 23(4) of Directive 2004/109/EC of 15 December 2004.

The exemption in the first subparagraph shall be subject to the following conditions:

a) the management report of the exempted subsidiary undertaking contains all of the following information:
   i. the name and registered office of the parent undertaking that reports information at group level in accordance with this Article or in a manner equivalent to the sustainability reporting standards adopted pursuant to Article 29b of this Directive, as determined in accordance with an implementing act on the equivalence of sustainability reporting standards adopted pursuant to the third subparagraph of Article 23(4) of Directive 2004/109/EC;
   ii. the weblinks to the consolidated management report of the parent undertaking or, where applicable, to the consolidated sustainability reporting of the parent undertaking, as referred to in the first subparagraph of this paragraph, and to the assurance opinion referred to in point (aa) of the second subparagraph of Article 34(1) of this Directive or to the assurance opinion referred to in point (b) of this subparagraph;
   iii. the information that the undertaking is exempted from the obligations set out in paragraphs 1 to 4 of this Article;
b) if the parent undertaking is established in a third country, its consolidated sustainability reporting and the assurance opinion on the consolidated sustainability reporting, expressed by one or more person(s) or firm(s) authorized to give an opinion on the assurance of sustainability reporting under the law governing that parent undertaking, are published in accordance with Article 30 of this Directive, and in accordance with the law of the Member State by which the exempted subsidiary undertaking is governed;
c) if the parent undertaking is established in a third country, the disclosures laid down in Article 8 of Regulation (EU) 2020/852 of 18 June 2020,[23] covering the activities carried out by the exempted subsidiary undertaking established in the Union and its subsidiary undertakings, are included in the management report of the exempted subsidiary

[23] See additional text No. 11, p. 28.

undertaking, or in the consolidated sustainability reporting carried out by the parent undertaking established in a third country.

The Member State by whose national law the exempted subsidiary undertaking is governed may require that the consolidated management report or, where applicable, the consolidated sustainability report, of the parent undertaking is published in a language that that Member State accepts, and that any necessary translation into such language is provided. Any translation that has not been certified shall include a statement to that effect.

Undertakings which are exempted from preparing a management report in accordance with Article 37[24] shall not be obliged to provide the information referred to in points (a)(i) to (iii) of the second subparagraph of this paragraph, provided that such undertakings publish the consolidated management report in accordance with Article 37.

For the purposes of the first subparagraph of this paragraph, and where Article 10 of Regulation (EU) No 575/2013 applies, credit institutions referred to in point (b) of the first subparagraph of Article 1(3) of this Directive that are permanently affiliated to a central body which supervises them under the conditions laid down in Article 10 of Regulation (EU) No 575/2013 shall be treated as subsidiary undertakings of that central body.

For the purposes of the first subparagraph of this paragraph, insurance undertakings referred to in point (a) of the first subparagraph of Article 1(3) of this Directive that are part of a group, on the basis of financial relationships as referred to in point (c)(ii) of Article 212(1) of Directive 2009/138/EC,[25] and which are subject to group supervision in accordance with points (a) to (c) of Article 213(2) of that Directive[26] shall be treated as subsidiary undertakings of the parent undertaking of that group.

10. The exemption laid down in paragraph 9 shall also apply to public-interest entities subject to the requirements of this Article, with the exception of large undertakings which are public-interest entities defined in point (a) of point (1) of Article 2 of this Directive.

---

24 'Exemption for subsidiary undertakings'; see additional text No. 12, p. 28.

25 See additional text No. 13, p. 29.

26 It outlines the circumstances in which group supervision applies to parent companies and their subsidiaries within the European Union. This article establishes rules for the consolidation of financial statements for groups of companies, ensuring that the financial position and performance of the group as a whole are accurately reflected.

I. ADDITIONAL TEXTS

A. ADDITIONAL TEXT NO. 7

Regulation (EU) 2021/1119 of the European Parliament and of the Council of 30 June 2021, Climate neutrality regulation or European Climate Law, Article 1

This Regulation establishes a framework for the irreversible and gradual reduction of anthropogenic greenhouse gas emissions by sources and enhancement of removals by sinks regulated in Union law.

This Regulation sets out a binding objective of climate neutrality in the Union by 2050 in pursuit of the long-term temperature goal set out in point (a) of Article 2(1) of the Paris Agreement, and provides a framework for achieving progress in pursuit of the global adaptation goal established in Article 7 of the Paris Agreement. This Regulation also sets out a binding Union target of a net domestic reduction in greenhouse gas emissions for 2030.

This Regulation applies to anthropogenic emissions by sources and removals by sinks of the greenhouse gases listed in Part 2 of Annex V to Regulation (EU) 2018/1999.

B. ADDITIONAL TEXT NO. 8

Regulation (EU) No 575/2013 of the European Parliament and of the Council of 26 June 2013, Capital Requirements Regulation (CRR), Article 4(1), point (145)

(145) 'small and non-complex institution' means an institution that meets all the following conditions:

a) it is not a large institution;
b) the total value of its assets on an individual basis or, where applicable, on a consolidated basis in accordance with this Regulation and Directive 2013/36/EU is on average equal to or less than the threshold of EUR 5 billion over the four-year period immediately preceding the current annual reporting period; Member States may lower that threshold;
c) it is not subject to any obligations, or is subject to simplified obligations, in relation to recovery and resolution planning in accordance with Article 4 of Directive 2014/59/EU;
d) its trading book business is classified as small within the meaning of Article 94(1);

e) the total value of its derivative positions held with trading intent does not exceed 2% of its total on- and off-balance-sheet assets and the total value of its overall derivative positions does not exceed 5%, both calculated in accordance with Article 273a(3);

f) more than 75% of both the institution's consolidated total assets and liabilities, excluding in both cases the intragroup exposures, relate to activities with counterparties located in the European Economic Area;[27]

g) the institution does not use internal models to meet the prudential requirements in accordance with this Regulation except for subsidiaries using internal models developed at the group level, provided that the group is subject to the disclosure requirements laid down in Article 433a or 433c on a consolidated basis;

h) the institution has not communicated to the competent authority an objection to being classified as a small and non-complex institution;

i) the competent authority has not decided that the institution is not to be considered a small and non-complex institution on the basis of an analysis of its size, interconnectedness, complexity or risk profile;

C. ADDITIONAL TEXT NO. 9

Directive 2009/138/EC of the European Parliament and of the Council of 25 November 2009, Solvency II, Article 13, point (2) and point (5)

13. (2) 'captive insurance undertaking' means an insurance undertaking, owned either by a financial undertaking other than an insurance or reinsurance undertaking or a group of insurance or reinsurance undertakings within the meaning of Article 212(1)(c) or by a non-financial undertaking, the purpose of which is to provide insurance cover exclusively for the risks of the undertaking or undertakings to which it belongs or of an undertaking or undertakings of the group of which it is a member;

[...]

27 In January 2025, the point f) of this article will be replaced by the following sentence: 'the institution's consolidated assets or liabilities relating to activities with counterparties located in the European Economic Area, excluding intragroup exposures in the European Economic Area, exceed 75% of both the institution's consolidated total assets and liabilities, excluding in both cases the intragroup exposures'.

(5) 'captive reinsurance undertaking' means a reinsurance undertaking, owned either by a financial undertaking other than an insurance or reinsurance undertaking or a group of insurance or reinsurance undertakings within the meaning of Article 212(1)(c) or by a non-financial undertaking, the purpose of which is to provide reinsurance cover exclusively for the risks of the undertaking or undertakings to which it belongs or of an undertaking or undertakings of the group of which it is a member;

D. ADDITIONAL TEXT NO. 10

Directive 2013/34/EU of the European Parliament and of the Council of 26 June 2013, Accounting Directive, Article 29

1. The consolidated management report shall, as a minimum, in addition to any other information required under other provisions of this Directive, set out the information required by Articles 19 and 20, taking account of the essential adjustments resulting from the particular characteristics of a consolidated management report as compared to a management report in a way which facilitates the assessment of the position of the undertakings included in the consolidation taken as a whole.
2. The following adjustments to the information required by Articles 19 and 20 shall apply:
   a) in reporting details of own shares acquired, the consolidated management report shall indicate the number and nominal value or, in the absence of a nominal value, the accounting par value of all of the parent undertaking's shares held by that parent undertaking, by subsidiary undertakings of that parent undertaking or by a person acting in his own name but on behalf of any of those undertakings. A Member State may permit or require the disclosure of those particulars in the notes to the consolidated financial statements;
   b) in reporting on internal control and risk management systems, the corporate governance statement shall refer to the main features of the internal controls and risk management systems for the undertakings included in the consolidation, taken as a whole.
3. Where a consolidated management report is required in addition to the management report, the two reports may be presented as a single report.

E. ADDITIONAL TEXT NO. 11

Regulation (EU) 2020/852 of the European Parliament and of the Council of 18 June 2020, Taxonomy Regulation, Article 8

1. Any undertaking which is subject to an obligation to publish non-financial information pursuant to Article 19a or Article 29a of Directive 2013/34/EU shall include in its non-financial statement or consolidated non-financial statement information on how and to what extent the undertaking's activities are associated with economic activities that qualify as environmentally sustainable under Articles 3 and 9 of this Regulation.
2. In particular, non-financial undertakings shall disclose the following:
   a) the proportion of their turnover derived from products or services associated with economic activities that qualify as environmentally sustainable under Articles 3 and 9; and
   b) the proportion of their capital expenditure and the proportion of their operating expenditure related to assets or processes associated with economic activities that qualify as environmentally sustainable under Articles 3 and 9.
3. If an undertaking publishes non-financial information pursuant to Article 19a or Article 29a of Directive 2013/34/EU in a separate report in accordance with Article 19a(4) or Article 29a(4) of that Directive, the information referred to in paragraphs 1 and 2 of this Article shall be published in that separate report.
4. The Commission shall adopt a delegated act in accordance with Article 23 to supplement paragraphs 1 and 2 of this Article to specify the content and presentation of the information to be disclosed pursuant to those paragraphs, including the methodology to be used in order to comply with them, taking into account the specificities of both financial and non-financial undertakings and the technical screening criteria established pursuant to this Regulation. The Commission shall adopt that delegated act by 1 June 2021.

F. ADDITIONAL TEXT NO. 12

Directive 2013/34/EU of the European Parliament and of the Council of 26 June 2013, Accounting Directive, Article 37

Notwithstanding the provisions of Directives 2009/101/EC and 2012/30/EU, a Member State shall not be required to apply the provisions of this Directive concerning the content, auditing and publication of the annual financial statements and the management report to undertakings governed by their national laws which are subsidiary undertakings, where the following conditions are fulfilled:

1) the parent undertaking is subject to the laws of a Member State;
2) all shareholders or members of the subsidiary undertaking have, in respect of each financial year in which the exemption is applied, declared their agreement to the exemption from such obligation;
3) the parent undertaking has declared that it guarantees the commitments entered into by the subsidiary undertaking;
4) the declarations referred to in points (2) and (3) of this Article are published by the subsidiary undertaking as laid down by the laws of the Member State in accordance with Chapter 2 of Directive 2009/101/EC;
5) the subsidiary undertaking is included in the consolidated financial statements drawn up by the parent undertaking in accordance with this Directive;
6) the exemption is disclosed in the notes to the consolidated financial statements drawn up by the parent undertaking; and
7) the consolidated financial statements referred to in point (5) of this Article, the consolidated management report, and the audit report are published for the subsidiary undertaking as laid down by the laws of the Member State in accordance with Chapter 2 of Directive 2009/101/EC.

G. ADDITIONAL TEXT NO. 13

Directive 2009/138/EC of the European Parliament and the Council of 25 November 2009, Solvency II, Article 212(1), point (c)(ii)

1. For the purposes of this Title, the following definitions shall apply: [...]
   c) 'group' means a group of undertakings that: [...]
      ii. is based on the establishment, contractually or otherwise, of strong and sustainable financial relationships among those undertakings, and that may include mutual or mutual-type associations, provided that:
         - one of those undertakings effectively exercises, through centralised coordination, a dominant influence over the decisions, including financial decisions, of the other undertakings that are part of the group; and,
         - the establishment and dissolution of such relationships for the purposes of this Title are subject to prior approval by the group supervisor,

where the undertaking exercising the centralised coordination shall be considered as the parent undertaking, and the other undertakings shall be considered as subsidiaries;

II. COMMENTS

A. FIRST COMMENT

1. Policy Context: Improving the World of Sustainable Finance

In its Communication of 8 March 2018 entitled 'Action Plan: Financing Sustainable Growth' (the 'Action Plan on Financing Sustainable Growth'), the Commission set out measures to achieve the following objectives: reorient capital flows towards sustainable investment in order to achieve sustainable and inclusive growth, manage financial risks stemming from climate change, resource depletion, environmental degradation and social issues, and foster transparency and long-termism in financial and economic activity.

Nonetheless, there is ample evidence that the sustainability information that companies currently report is not sufficient. They often omit information that investors and other stakeholders deem important. Reported information can be hard to compare from company to company, and users of the information, such as investors, are often unsure whether they can trust it. The disclosure by certain categories of undertakings of relevant, comparable and reliable sustainability information is a prerequisite for meeting those objectives.

Article 1 of the CSRD introduces new articles (19a and 29a) in the Accounting Directive, prescribing with various levels of granularity what information shall be disclosed, on environmental, social and governance matters.

More specifically, they require companies of a certain size category,[28] either at subsidiary level (Article 19a) or at consolidated parent-company level (Article 29a), to disclose information and clear time-bound targets set by the undertaking on five sustainability reporting areas:

1. Business model;
2. Policies, including the due-diligence processes implemented;
3. The outcome of these policies;
4. Risks and risk management;
5. Key performance indicators relevant to the disclosures.

[28] See Arts. 1 and 2, pp. 3 and 9.

2. *The 'Double Materiality' Principle*

Societal expectations have grown exponentially around sustainability issues in the last decade, and this has resulted in an increased global push for companies to consider and report both their impacts on their environment as well as how sustainability issues impact companies' financial well-being. The European Union has dubbed this concept 'Double Materiality'. As a result, a global corporate reporting regime is emerging in which sustainability impact reporting and strengthened financial reporting are mandated on an equal footing, as two key perspectives managed with the same rigour:

- Perspective 1 – Reporting on companies' impacts on society and the environment, and their contributions towards sustainable development.
- Perspective 2 – Reporting on sustainability-related financial disclosures addressing the financial implications of sustainability issues.

Or in other words, this requires undertakings to report both on the impacts of their activities on people and the environment, and on how sustainability matters affect them.

The fitness check on corporate reporting shows that those two perspectives are often not well understood or applied. This article therefore aims to clarify that undertakings should consider each materiality perspective in its own right, and should disclose information that is material from both perspectives as well as information that is material from only one perspective.

3. *Information on the Value Chain*

The sustainability statement of the company needs to cover all significant impacts, risks, and opportunities (IROs) related to all its activities, including IROs stemming from its business relationships across the entire value chain. This relationship extends beyond direct contractual connections. While the disclosure of value-chain information is not obligatory for all datapoints, it is required when associated with significant IROs beyond the company's own operations. The materiality assessment should identify significant IROs within the value chain, focusing on their likely occurrence across various aspects like geographies, activities, suppliers, and customers.

There is a transition period of three years for the reporting of sustainability information of value-chain partners, with the aim of easing the initial reporting for large companies and to help SMEs in the value chain to prepare it. During this transition period, the following conditions apply:

- if not all the necessary information regarding its value chain is available, it is sufficient that the reporting company explain the efforts made to obtain the necessary information about its value chain, the reasons why not all the necessary information could be obtained, and its plans to retrieve them in the future;

- when disclosing information on policies, actions and targets, the reporting company may limit value-chain information to that available in-house and publicly; and
- when disclosing metrics, the company is not required to include value-chain information, except for datapoints derived from other EU legislation.[29]

4. *Trade Secrets*

The CSRD does not aim 'to require undertakings to disclose intellectual capital, intellectual property, know-how or the results of innovation that would qualify as trade secrets as defined in Directive (EU) 2016/943 of the European Parliament and of the Council. Reporting requirements provided for in this amending Directive should therefore be without prejudice to Directive (EU) 2016/943'.[30]

5. *SMEs' Opt Out*

Listed SMEs on regulated markets and small listed non-complex credit institutions which are public-interest entities, and captive insurance or reinsurance companies, must apply these new rules as of the fiscal year 2026.

However, the legislator considered they should be given sufficient time to prepare for the application of the provisions requiring sustainability reporting, due to their smaller size and more limited resources, and taking account of the difficult economic circumstances created by the COVID-19 pandemic. Therefore, 'for a transitional period of two years, small and medium-sized undertakings whose securities are admitted to trading on a regulated market in the Union should have the possibility of opting-out from the sustainability reporting requirements laid down in this amending Directive, provided they briefly state in their management report why the sustainability information has not been provided'.[31]

6. *Conditions for Exemption for Subsidiaries' Reporting*

The CSRD extends the existing rules that govern the disclosure and consolidation of sustainability information to environmental, social, human rights, and governance topics. Both financial and sustainability information shall now appear in the same consolidated management report, although the sustainability statement shall be presented in a dedicated section.

---

29 See additional text No. 15, p. 58.

30 CSRD, extract from Recital 34.

31 CSRD, extract from Recital 21.

The Directive further specifies that subsidiary undertakings are exempted from the obligation to include a full individual sustainability statement in their own management report, if they are included in the consolidated management report of another (parent) company drawn up in accordance with the CSRD and the ESRS.

In practice, this means that parent companies must include subsidiaries in their consolidated sustainability statement, and that such consolidated subsidiaries may use the exemption or may issue an individual sustainability statement in their own management report, in addition to being consolidated.

Therefore, a subsidiary within the scope of the CSRD needs to provide a sustainability statement and issue an individual report, or have this information consolidated at parent-company level – such as with an EU holding company. In this case, the subsidiary is exempted from publishing a stand-alone report. This exemption does not apply to PIEs that are large, listed companies on an EU regulated market. For those, whether they are consolidated by their parent company or not, a sustainability statement in their own management report is still required.

The CSRD explicitly states that the exemption regime for consolidated sustainability reporting operates independently from the exemption to prepare consolidated financial statements and a consolidated management report. This, for instance, means that a holding based in the EU and that consolidates financial reports for its subsidiaries may not consolidate sustainability reports.

If there are significant differences between the sustainability risks or impacts of the group and those of its subsidiaries, the parent company should provide, in the consolidated sustainability statement, an adequate understanding of the risks or impacts of its subsidiaries – including information on their due diligence processes (where appropriate).

During the transposition process by Member States, national authorities have the discretion to restrict the use of reporting exemptions or to mandate distinct disclosures at entity or country level. This might involve obligating companies within the country to submit standalone reports.

To sum up, EU subsidiaries can be exempted from publishing a management report that includes sustainability information unless they are large, listed public-interest entities.

7. The Specific Case of Subsidiaries with Parent Companies Based outside the EU

A distinctive form of the subsidiary exemption is temporarily applicable to EU subsidiaries or subgroups with a parent company headquartered outside the EU. Until 2030, these companies may be exempted from individual reporting requirements if they are incorporated into a report using European

Sustainability Reporting Standards (ESRS)[32] and 'artificial consolidation' has been done, meaning that the EU subsidiaries and subgroups are consolidated. The entity responsible for consolidating other EU-based subsidiaries is the one with the highest turnover within the EU. The purpose of this transitional provision is to reduce the burden for the non-EU groups that do not have a single EU-based holding entity that controls the group's EU entities.

The ultimate parent companies that are not based in the EU may also consolidate their EU subsidiaries in a global sustainability statement. However, such consolidation exempts the EU subsidiaries from the obligation to produce their own sustainability statements only if the global consolidated statement is drawn up in accordance with the ESRS, or in an equivalent manner.

8. *The Taxonomy Regulation*[33]

Article 3 of Regulation (EU) 2020/852 outlines the objectives of the text, which include establishing a framework for determining whether an economic activity is environmentally sustainable, providing market participants with clarity and transparency on the environmental sustainability of economic activities, and promoting private sector investment in sustainable projects.

An economic activity is environmentally sustainable if, notably, it contributes substantially to one or more of the environmental objectives pursued by the directive and does not significantly harm any of the environmental objective and complies with technical screening criteria that have been established by the Commission.

In its Article 9, the Regulation establishes the environmental objectives pursued by the text which are:

- climate change mitigation;
- climate change adaptation;
- the sustainable use and protection of water and marine resources;
- the transition to a circular economy;
- pollution prevention and control; and
- the protection and restoration of biodiversity and ecosystems.

'Given the specific technical details needed to assess the environmental impact of an economic activity and the fast-changing nature of both science and technology, the criteria for environmentally sustainable economic activities should be adapted regularly to reflect such changes. For the criteria to be up to date, based on scientific evidence and input from experts as well as relevant stakeholders, the conditions for 'substantial contribution' and 'significant harm' should be specified in more detail for different economic activities and

---

32 See additionnal text No. 15, p. 58, and comment p. 67.

33 See comment p. 70.

should be updated regularly. For that purpose, granular and calibrated technical screening criteria for the different economic activities should be established by the Commission based on technical input from a multi-stakeholder platform on sustainable finance.'[34]

'An economic activity should not qualify as environmentally sustainable if it causes more harm to the environment than the benefits it brings. The technical screening criteria should identify the minimum requirements necessary to avoid significant harm to other objectives, including by building on any minimum requirements laid down pursuant to Union law. When establishing and updating the technical screening criteria, the Commission should ensure that they are based on available scientific evidence that they take into account life-cycle considerations, including existing life-cycle assessments, and that they are updated regularly.'[35]

The Technical Group on Sustainable Finance (TEG), assisted the European Commission in developing technical screening criteria for environmentally sustainable economic activities. It played a crucial role in the implementation of the taxonomy framework. It has been replaced by the Platform on Sustainable Finance in 2020.

B. SECOND COMMENT

Supervision of Financial Institutions by Central Bodies

The supervision of financial institutions in the European Union is primarily managed by several central bodies: the European Central Bank (ECB) oversees significant banks in the Eurozone under the Single Supervisory Mechanism (SSM); the European Banking Authority (EBA) ensures consistent prudential regulation across the banking sector; the European Securities and Markets Authority (ESMA) regulates securities markets and credit rating agencies; the European Insurance and Occupational Pensions Authority (EIOPA) supervises insurance and pensions sectors; and the European Systemic Risk Board (ESRB) monitors and assesses systemic risks to ensure financial stability. These institutions collectively ensure the stability, transparency, and integrity of the EU's financial system. Article 10 of the Capital Requirements Regulation addresses the waiver for credit institutions permanently affiliated to a central body. This article outlines the conditions under which competent authorities may waive the application of certain requirements of the regulation to credit institutions affiliated to a central body which supervises them.

---

34 Regulation (EU) 2020/852, Taxonomy Regulation, Recital 38.

35 Regulation (EU) 2020/852, Taxonomy Regulation, extract from Recital 40.

MATERIALITY ASSESSMENT OF SUSTAINABILITY DATA

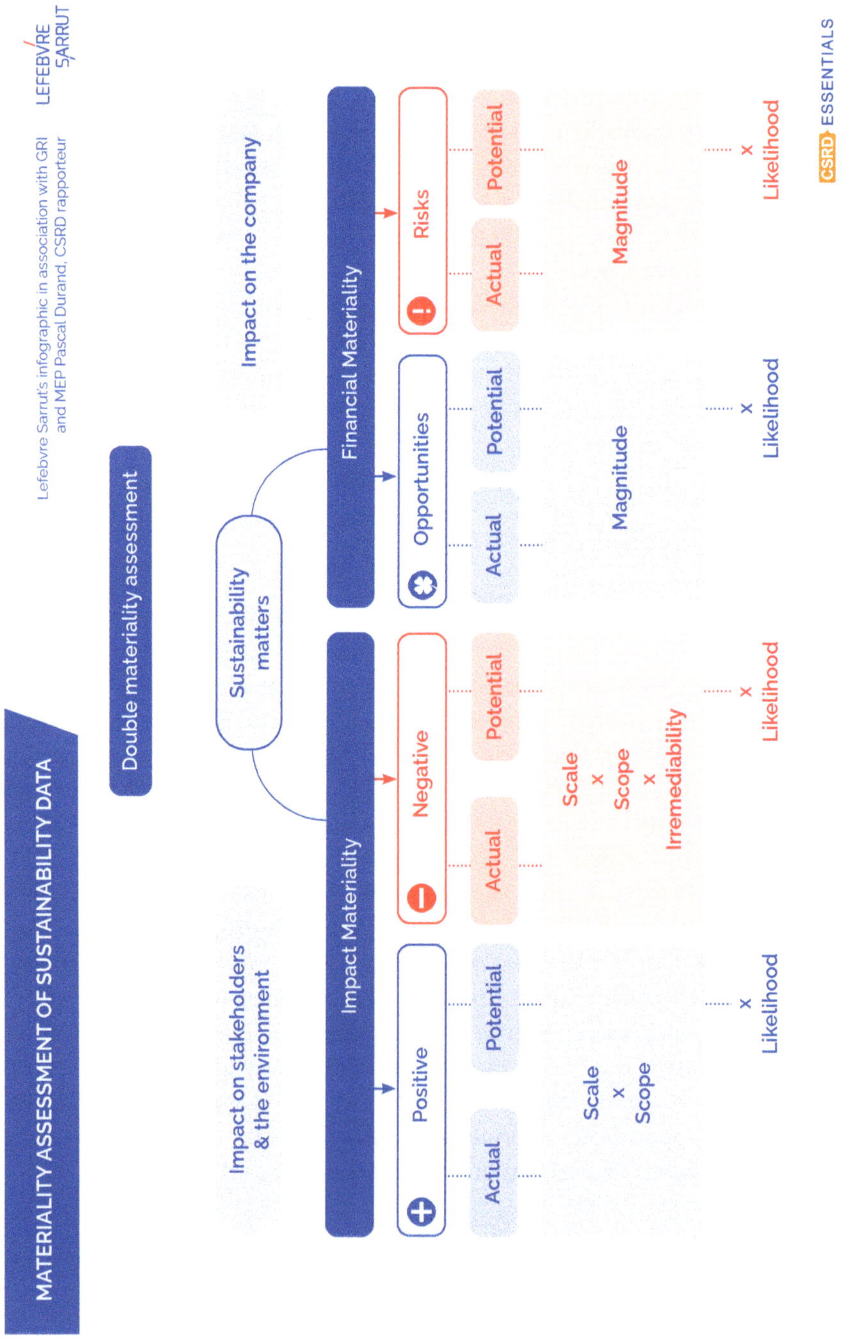

ARTICLE 20
CORPORATE GOVERNANCE STATEMENT

Extract

[1. Undertakings referred to in point (1)(a) of Article 2[36] shall include a corporate governance statement in their management report. That statement shall be included as a specific section of the management report and shall contain at least the following information:

(a) a reference to the following, where applicable:
   (i) the corporate governance code to which the undertaking is subject,
   (ii) the corporate governance code which the undertaking may have voluntarily decided to apply,
   (iii) all relevant information about the corporate governance practices applied over and above the requirements of national law.
   (iv) Where reference is made to a corporate governance code referred to in points (i) or (ii), the undertaking shall also indicate where the relevant texts are publicly available. Where reference is made to the information referred to in point (iii), the undertaking shall make details of its corporate governance practices publicly available;

(b) where an undertaking, in accordance with national law, departs from a corporate governance code referred to in points (a)(i) or (ii), an explanation by the undertaking as to which parts of the corporate governance code it departs from and the reasons for doing so; where the undertaking has decided not to refer to any provisions of a corporate governance code referred to in points (a)(i) or (ii), it shall explain its reasons for not doing so;

(c) a description of the main features of the undertaking's internal control and risk management systems in relation to the financial reporting process;

(d) the information required by points (c), (d), (f), (h) and (i) of Article 10(1) of Directive 2004/25/EC of the European Parliament and of the Council

---

36 Public-interest entities governed by the law of a Member State and whose transferable securities are admitted to trading on a regulated market of a Member State.

of 21 April 2004 on takeover bids,[37] where the undertaking is subject to that Directive;]

[...]

(g) a description of the diversity policy applied in relation to the undertaking's administrative, management and supervisory bodies with regard to gender and other aspects such as, age, disabilities or educational and professional background, the objectives of that diversity policy, how it has been implemented and the results in the reporting period. If no such policy is applied, the statement shall contain an explanation as to why that is the case.

Undertakings subject to Article 19a shall be deemed to have complied with the obligation laid down in point (g) of the first subparagraph of this paragraph where they include the information required under that point as part of their sustainability reporting and a reference thereto is included in the corporate governance statement.

[...]

I. ADDITIONAL TEXTS

A. ADDITIONAL TEXT NO. 14

Directive 2004/25/EC of the European Parliament and of the Council of 21 April 2004, Takeover bids Directive, Article 10(1), points (c), (d), (f), (h) and (i)

1. Member States shall ensure that companies as referred to in Article 1(1) publish detailed information on the following:

[...]

(c) significant direct and indirect shareholdings (including indirect shareholdings through pyramid structures and cross-shareholdings) within the meaning of Article 85 of Directive 2001/34/EC;

(d) the holders of any securities with special control rights and a description of those rights;

[...]

(f) any restrictions on voting rights, such as limitations of the voting rights of holders of a given percentage or number of votes, deadlines for exercising voting rights, or systems whereby, with the company's cooperation, the financial rights attaching to securities are separated from the holding of securities;

[37] See additional text No. 14, p. 38.

[...]

(h) the rules governing the appointment and replacement of board members and the amendment of the articles of association;

(i) the powers of board members, and in particular the power to issue or buy back shares;

II. COMMENTS

A. FIRST COMMENT

Corporate Governance Statement

'Article 20 of Directive 2013/34/EU requires undertakings whose securities are admitted to trading on a regulated market in the Union to include a corporate governance statement in their management report, which has to contain, among other information, a description of the diversity policy applied by the undertaking in relation to its administrative, management and supervisory bodies. Article 20 of Directive 2013/34/EU leaves flexibility to undertakings to decide what aspects of diversity they report on. It does not explicitly oblige undertakings to include information on any particular aspect of diversity. In order to progress towards a more gender-balanced participation in economic decision-making, it is necessary to ensure that undertakings whose securities are admitted to trading on a regulated market in the Union always report on their gender diversity policies and the implementation thereof. However, to avoid an unnecessary administrative burden, such undertakings should have the possibility of reporting some of the information required by Article 20 of Directive 2013/34/EU alongside other sustainability information. If they decide to do so, the corporate governance statement should include a reference to the undertaking's sustainability reporting, and the information required under Article 20 of Directive 2013/34/EU should remain subject to the assurance requirements of the corporate governance statement.'[38]

B. SECOND COMMENT

The Corporate Governance Code

The Corporate governance code encompasses a set of guidelines or principles established by regulatory bodies or industry associations to govern how

[38] CSRD, Recital 58.

corporations should be managed and overseen. These codes typically address areas such as board composition, risk management, transparency, shareholder rights, and ethical standards. While not all are legally binding, they serve as important benchmarks for promoting transparency, accountability, and the protection of stakeholders' interests within companies, aiming to foster trust and confidence in corporate decision-making processes. Compliance with these codes is often voluntary, though companies may be required to disclose their adherence levels in their annual reports or regulatory filings, underscoring their significance in shaping corporate governance practices.

C. THIRD COMMENT

Information on Takeover Bids

The information required by the Directive 2004/25/EC (Article 6) on takeover bids aims to ensure transparency and provide shareholders and other stakeholders with relevant information to make informed decisions regarding takeover bids.

It requires the disclosure of the number and percentage of voting rights held in the target company by the bidder, including any financial instruments that give access to shares with voting rights.

It mandates the disclosure of any agreements, arrangements, or understandings between the bidder and persons acting in concert with them regarding the acquisition of voting rights in the target company.

It requires the disclosure of the bidder's intentions regarding the target company's future business activities, including any significant changes in the company's structure or employment.

It mandates the disclosure of any conditions attached to the bid, including regulatory, financial, or material conditions that could affect the bid's completion.

It requires the disclosure of the bidder's financing arrangements for the proposed takeover bid, including details of any financing facilities or agreements secured to fund the acquisition.

ARTICLE 23
EXEMPTIONS FROM CONSOLIDATION

Extract

[1. Small groups shall be exempted from the obligation to draw up consolidated financial statements and a consolidated management report, except where any affiliated undertaking is a public-interest entity.

2. Member States may exempt medium-sized groups from the obligation to draw up consolidated financial statements and a consolidated management report, except where any affiliated undertaking is a public-interest entity.

3. Notwithstanding paragraphs 1 and 2 of this Article, a Member State shall, in the following cases, exempt from the obligation to draw up consolidated financial statements and a consolidated management report any parent undertaking (the exempted undertaking) governed by its national law which is also a subsidiary undertaking, including a public-interest entity unless that public-interest entity falls under point (1)(a) of Article 2,[39] the own parent undertaking of which is governed by the law of a Member State and:

   (a) the parent undertaking of the exempted undertaking holds all of the shares in the exempted undertaking. The shares in the exempted undertaking held by members of its administrative, management or supervisory bodies pursuant to a legal obligation or an obligation in its memorandum or articles of association shall be ignored for this purpose; or

   (b) the parent undertaking of the exempted undertaking holds 90% or more of the shares in the exempted undertaking and the remaining shareholders in or members of the exempted undertaking have approved the exemption.

4. The exemptions referred to in paragraph 3 shall fulfill all of the following conditions:

   (a) the exempted undertaking and, without prejudice to paragraph 9, all of its subsidiary undertakings are consolidated in the financial statements of a larger body of undertakings, the parent undertaking of which is governed by the law of a Member State;]

---

39 Listed companies on regulated markets of EU Member States.

(b) the consolidated financial statements referred to in point (a) and the consolidated management report of the larger body of undertakings are drawn up by the parent undertaking of that body, in accordance with the law of the Member State by which that parent undertaking is governed, in accordance with this Directive, with the exception of the requirements laid down in Article 29a,[40] or in accordance with international accounting standards adopted in accordance with Regulation (EC) No 1606/2002;[41]

[...]

[8. Without prejudice to paragraphs 1, 2, 3 and 5 of this Article, a Member State which provides for exemptions under paragraphs 3 and 5 of this Article [other cases of exemption] may also exempt from the obligation to draw up consolidated financial statements and a consolidated management report any parent undertaking (the exempted undertaking) governed by its national law which is also a subsidiary undertaking, including a public-interest entity unless that public-interest entity falls under point (1)(a) of Article 2, the parent undertaking of which is not governed by the law of a Member State, if all of the following conditions are fulfilled:

(a) the exempted undertaking and, without prejudice to paragraph 9 [this paragraph outlines conditions exempting certain undertakings, including public-interest entities, from inclusion in consolidated financial statements. Exemptions apply in cases of disproportionate expense or undue delay in obtaining necessary information for consolidation, when shares are held solely for resale, or when severe, long-term restrictions impede the parent company's control over assets or management, or hinder unified management in specified relationships], all of its subsidiary undertakings are consolidated in the financial statements of a larger body of undertakings;

(b) the consolidated financial statements referred to in point (a) and, where appropriate, the consolidated management report are drawn up:]

(i) in accordance with this Directive, with the exception of the requirements laid down in Article 29a,

[...]

---

40 See also comment p. 32.

41 Application of international accounting standards; see comment p. 107.

(iii) in a manner equivalent to consolidated financial statements and consolidated management reports drawn up in accordance with this Directive, with the exception of the requirements laid down in Article 29a;[42] or

[...]

COMMENTS

EQUIVALENCE OF REPORTING STANDARDS

The equivalence between EU and other jurisdictions concerning the use of financial and sustainability standards is essential for the comparability and consistency of financial and sustainability reporting globally. The European Commission assesses the equivalence of third-country accounting standards with IFRS to determine whether financial statements prepared under these standards provide a level of transparency and reliability comparable to those prepared under International Financial Reporting Standards (IFRS). Some of the countries that have been granted equivalence with the EU in terms of accounting standards include the United States (under the US Generally Accepted Accounting Principles, or US GAAP), Japan, Canada, People's Republic of China and various others.

In addition, the CSRD provides the European Commission with the possibility to allow third-country companies within the scope of the CSRD, or non-EU parent companies of EU subsidiaries (such as those based in the US or the UK), to use sustainability standards equivalent to the ESRS. In that case, the European Commission will need to grant an equivalence status to those jurisdictions first.

If deemed equivalent, companies from these jurisdictions may use their local standards for sustainability reporting purposes in the EU, reducing the need for reconciliation and facilitating cross-border investments.

---

42 The CSRD provides the European Commission with the possibility to allow third country companies within the scope of the CSRD, or non-EU parent companies of EU subsidiaries (such as those based in the US or the UK), to use sustainability standards equivalent to the ESRS.

ARTICLE 29A
CONSOLIDATED SUSTAINABILITY REPORTING

1. Parent undertakings of a large group as referred to in Article 3(7)[43] shall include in the consolidated management report information necessary to understand the group's impacts on sustainability matters,[44] and information necessary to understand how sustainability matters affect the group's development, performance and position.[45]
   The information referred to in the first subparagraph shall be clearly identifiable within the consolidated management report, through a dedicated section of the consolidated management report.
2. The information referred to in paragraph 1 shall contain:[46]
   (a) a brief description of the group's business model and strategy, including:
      (i) the resilience of the group's business model and strategy in relation to risks related to sustainability matters;
      (ii) the opportunities for the group related to sustainability matters;
      (iii) the plans of the group, including implementing actions and related financial and investment plans, to ensure that its business model and strategy are compatible with the transition to a sustainable economy and with the limiting of global warming to 1,5 °C in line with the Paris Agreement and the objective of achieving climate neutrality by 2050 as established in Regulation (EU) 2021/1119[47] and where relevant, the exposure of the group to coal-, oil- and gas-related activities;

---

[43] Art. 3(7): 'Large groups shall be groups consisting of parent and subsidiary undertakings to be included in a consolidation and which, on a consolidated basis, exceed the limits of at least two of the three following criteria on the balance sheet date of the parent undertaking: (a) balance sheet total: EUR 25 000 000; (b) net turnover: EUR 50 000 000; (c) average number of employees during the financial year: 250.'

[44] Environmental, social and employee matters, respect for human rights, anti-corruption and anti-bribery matters as well as other specific entities' governance matters. These are more precisely defined in accordance with the European Sustainability Reporting Standards (ESRS) (see additional text No. 15, p. 58). For example, it can be diversity policies or child labour when it comes to governance and human rights respectively.

[45] Double materiality principle; see comment p. 31.

[46] See comment p. 30.

[47] See additional text No. 7, p. 25.

(iv) how the group's business model and strategy take account of the interests of the group's stakeholders and of the impacts of the group on sustainability matters;

(v) how the group's strategy has been implemented with regard to sustainability matters;

(b) a description of the time-bound targets related to sustainability matters set by the group, including, where appropriate, absolute greenhouse gas emission reduction targets at least for 2030 and 2050, a description of the progress the group has made towards achieving those targets, and a statement of whether the group's targets related to environmental factors are based on conclusive scientific evidence;

(c) a description of the role of the administrative, management and supervisory bodies with regard to sustainability matters, and of their expertise and skills in relation to fulfilling that role or the access such bodies have to such expertise and skills;

(d) a description of the group's policies in relation to sustainability matters;

(e) information about the existence of incentive schemes linked to sustainability matters which are offered to members of the administrative, management and supervisory bodies;

(f) a description of:

(i) the due diligence process implemented by the group with regard to sustainability matters, and, where applicable, in line with Union requirements on undertakings to conduct a due diligence process;

(ii) the principal actual or potential adverse impacts connected with the group's own operations and with its value chain, including its products and services, its business relationships and its supply chain, actions taken to identify and monitor those impacts, and other adverse impacts which the parent undertaking is required to identify pursuant to other Union requirements to conduct a due diligence process;

(iii) any actions taken by the group to prevent, mitigate, remediate or bring an end to actual or potential adverse impacts, and the result of such actions;

(g) any actions taken by the group to prevent, mitigate, remediate or bring an end to actual or potential adverse impacts, and the result of such actions;

(h) indicators relevant to the disclosures referred to in points (a) to (g).

Parent undertakings shall report the process carried out to identify the information that they have included in the consolidated management report in accordance with paragraph 1 of this Article. The information listed in the first subparagraph of this paragraph shall include information related to short-, medium- and long-term time horizons, as applicable.

3. Where applicable, the information referred to in paragraphs 1 and 2 shall contain information about the group's own operations and about its value chain, including its products and services, its business relationships and its supply chain.
   For the first three years of the application of the measures to be adopted by the Member States in accordance with Article 5(2) of Directive (EU) 2022/2464, and in the event that not all the necessary information regarding its value chain is available, the parent undertaking shall explain the efforts made to obtain the necessary information about its value chain, the reasons why not all of the necessary information could be obtained, and its plans to obtain the necessary information in the future.
   Where applicable, the information referred to in paragraphs 1 and 2 shall also include references to, and additional explanations of, the other information included in the consolidated management report in accordance with Article 29[48] of this Directive and the amounts reported in the consolidated financial statements.
   Member States may allow information relating to impending developments or matters in the course of negotiation to be omitted in exceptional cases where, in the duly justified opinion of the members of the administrative, management and supervisory bodies, acting within the competences assigned to them by national law and having collective responsibility for that opinion, the disclosure of such information would be seriously prejudicial to the commercial position of the group, provided that such omission does not prevent a fair and balanced understanding of the group's development, performance, and position, and the impact of its activity.[49]
4. Where the reporting undertaking identifies significant differences between the risks for, or impacts of, the group and the risks for, or impacts of, one or more of its subsidiary undertakings, the undertaking shall provide an adequate understanding of, as appropriate, the risks for, and impacts of, the subsidiary undertaking or subsidiary undertakings concerned.
   Undertakings shall indicate which subsidiary undertakings included in the consolidation are exempted from annual or consolidated sustainability reporting pursuant to Articles 19a(9) or 29a(8) respectively.
5. Parent undertakings shall report the information referred to in paragraphs 1 to 3 of this Article in accordance with the sustainability reporting standards adopted pursuant to Article 29b.
6. The management of the parent undertaking shall inform the workers' representatives at the appropriate level and discuss with them the relevant information and the means of obtaining and verifying sustainability information. The workers' representatives' opinion shall be communicated,

---

[48] See additional text No. 10, p. 27.
[49] See comment p. 32.

where applicable, to the relevant administrative, management or supervisory bodies.

7. A parent undertaking that complies with the requirements set out in paragraphs 1 to 5 of this Article shall be deemed to have complied with the requirements set out in the third subparagraph of Article 19(1) and Article 19a.
8. Provided that the conditions set out in the second subparagraph of this paragraph are met, a parent undertaking which is a subsidiary undertaking shall be exempted from the obligations set out in paragraphs 1 to 5 of this Article (the 'exempted parent undertaking') if such parent undertaking and its subsidiary undertakings are included in the consolidated management report of another undertaking, drawn up in accordance with Article 29 and this Article. A parent undertaking which is a subsidiary undertaking of a parent undertaking that is established in a third country shall also be exempted from the obligations set out in paragraphs 1 to 5 of this Article where such parent undertaking and its subsidiary undertakings are included in the consolidated sustainability reporting of that parent undertaking that is established in a third country and where that consolidated sustainability reporting is carried out in accordance with the sustainability reporting standards adopted pursuant to Article 29b or in a manner equivalent to those sustainability reporting standards, as determined in accordance with an implementing act on the equivalence of sustainability reporting standards adopted pursuant to the third subparagraph of Article 23(4) of Directive 2004/109/EC.

   The exemption in the first subparagraph shall be subject to the following conditions:

   (a) the management report of the exempted parent undertaking contains all of the following information:

      (i) the name and registered office of the parent undertaking that reports information at group level in accordance with this Article, or in a manner equivalent to the sustainability reporting standards adopted pursuant to Article 29b of this Directive, as determined in accordance with an implementing act on the equivalence of sustainability reporting standards adopted pursuant to the third subparagraph of Article 23(4) of Directive 2004/109/EC;

      (ii) the weblinks to the consolidated management report of the parent undertaking or, where applicable, to the consolidated sustainability reporting of the parent undertaking, as referred to in the first subparagraph of this paragraph, and to the assurance opinion referred to in point (aa) of the second subparagraph of Article 34(1) of this Directive or to the assurance opinion referred to in point (b) of this subparagraph;

(iii) the information that the parent undertaking is exempted from the obligations set out in paragraphs 1 to 5 of this Article;

(b) if the parent undertaking is established in a third country, its consolidated sustainability reporting and the assurance opinion, expressed by one or more person(s) or firm(s) authorized to give an opinion on the assurance of sustainability reporting under the national law governing the parent undertaking, are published in accordance with Article 30, and in accordance with the law of the Member State by which the exempted parent undertaking is governed;

(c) if the parent undertaking is established in a third country, the disclosures laid down in Article 8 of Regulation (EU) 2020/852,[50] covering the activities carried out by the subsidiary undertaking established in the Union and exempted from sustainability reporting on the basis of Article 19a(9) of this Directive, shall be included in the management report of the exempted parent undertaking, or in the consolidated sustainability reporting carried out by the parent undertaking established in a third country.

The Member State by whose national law the exempted parent undertaking is governed may require that the consolidated management report or, where applicable, the consolidated sustainability report of the parent undertaking is published in a language that Member State accepts, and that any necessary translation into such language is provided. Any translation that has not been certified shall include a statement to that effect.

Parent undertakings which are exempted from preparing a management report pursuant to Article 37[51] shall not be obliged to provide the information referred to in points (a)(i) to (a)(iii) of the second subparagraph of this paragraph, provided that such undertakings publish the consolidated management report in accordance with Article 37.

For the purposes of the first subparagraph of this paragraph, and where Article 10 of Regulation (EU) No 575/2013 applies, credit institutions referred to in point (b) of the first subparagraph of Article 1(3) of this Directive that are permanently affiliated to a central body which supervises them under the conditions laid down in Article 10 of Regulation (EU) No 575/2013[52] shall be treated as subsidiary undertakings of that central body.

For the purposes of the first subparagraph of this paragraph, insurance undertakings referred to in point (a) of the first subparagraph of Article 1(3) of this Directive that are part of a group, on the basis of financial relationships referred to in point (c)(ii) of Article 212(1) of Directive 2009/138/EC,[53] and which are subject to group supervision in accordance with points (a) to (c) of

[50] See additional text No. 11, p. 28.
[51] 'Exemption for subsidiary understankings'; see additional text No. 12, p. 28.
[52] See comment p. 35.
[53] See additional text No. 13, p. 29.

Article 213(2) of that Directive[54] shall be treated as subsidiary undertakings of the parent undertaking of that group.

9. The exemption laid down in paragraph 8 shall also apply to public-interest entities subject to the requirements of this Article, with the exception of large undertakings which are public-interest entities defined in point (a) of point (1) of Article 2[55] of this Directive.

COMMENTS

CONSOLIDATED SUSTAINABILITY REPORTING

While Article 19a requires large undertakings and public-interest entities to include a non-financial statement in their management reports – sustainability reporting – detailing policies, outcomes, risks, and KPIs related to environmental, social, and employee matters, respect for human rights, anti-corruption, and bribery issues, etc.;[56] Article 29a extends similar requirements to large groups, mandating that the consolidated management report includes non-financial information covering the entire group.

The requirements outlined for consolidated non-financial statements for parent undertakings of large groups also include those that are subsidiaries themselves. Specifically, if a parent undertaking is also a subsidiary, it is not required to prepare its own consolidated non-financial statement if the exempted group is included in the consolidated management report or a separate report of a larger group, unless it is a public-interest entity.

---

54 It outlines the circumstances in which group supervision applies to parent companies and their subsidiaries within the European Union.

55 Listed companies on regulated markets of EU Member States.

56 See comment p. 30.

CONSOLIDATION OF A PARENT COMPANY IN THE EU THAT HAS SUBSIDIARIES LISTED OR NOT

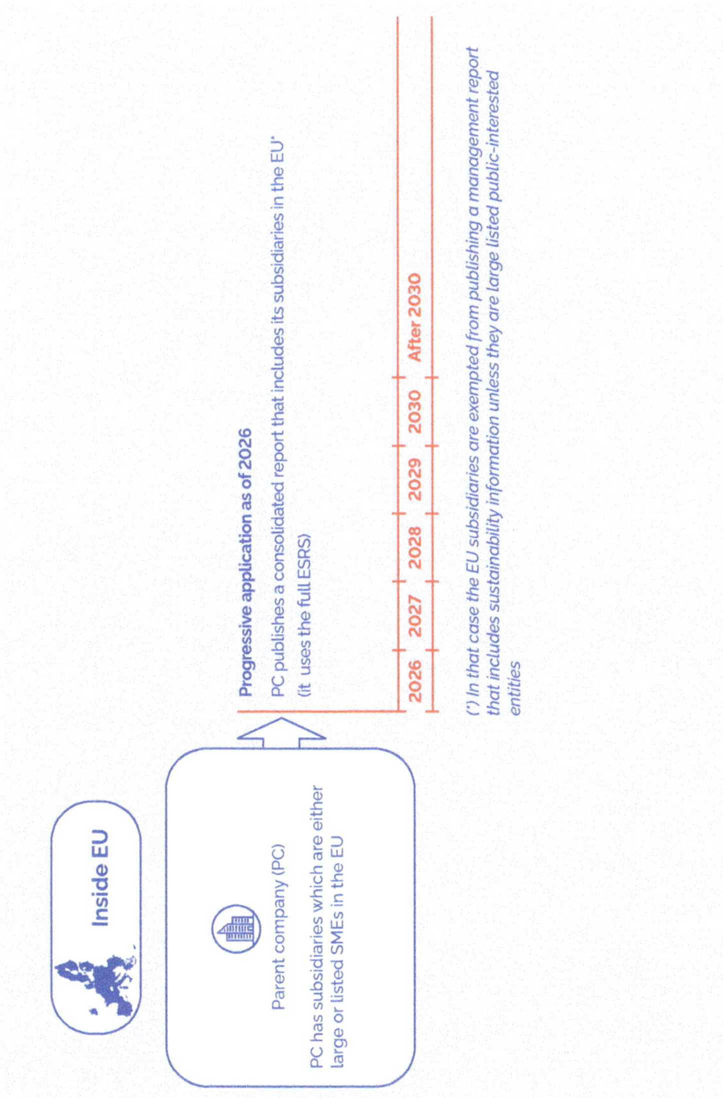

ARTICLE 29B
SUSTAINABILITY REPORTING STANDARDS

1. The Commission shall adopt delegated acts in accordance with Article 49 supplementing this Directive to provide for sustainability reporting standards. Those sustainability reporting standards shall specify the information that undertakings are to report in accordance with Articles 19a and 29a and, where relevant, shall specify the structure to be used to present that information.

   In the delegated acts referred to in the first subparagraph of this paragraph the Commission shall, by 30 June 2023,[57] specify the information that undertakings are to report in accordance with Article 19a (1)[58] and (2)[59] and Article 29a(1)[60] and (2)[61] where appropriate, which shall at least include the information that financial market participants subject to the disclosure obligations of Regulation (EU) 2019/2088[62] need in order to comply with those obligations.

   In the delegated acts referred to in the first subparagraph the Commission shall, by 30 June 2026 specify:

   (i) complementary information that undertakings are to report with regard to the sustainability matters and reporting areas listed in Article 19a(2), where necessary;

   (ii) information that undertakings are to report that is specific to the sector in which they operate.

---

57 See additional text No. 15, p. 58.

58 Art.19a(1): 'Large undertakings, and small and medium-sized undertakings, except micro undertakings, which are public-interest entities as defined in point (a) of point (1) of Article 2 shall include in the management report information necessary to understand the undertaking's impacts on sustainability matters, and information necessary to understand how sustainability matters affect the undertaking's development, performance and position.'

59 It lists the sustainability reporting disclosure requirements; see comment p. 30.

60 Art. 29a(1): 'Parent undertakings of a large group as referred to in Article 3(7) shall include in the consolidated management report information necessary to understand the group's impacts on sustainability matters, and information necessary to understand how sustainability matters affect the group's development, performance and position.'

61 It lists the sustainability reporting disclosure requirements; see comment p. 50.

62 See additional text No. 16, p. 61.

The Commission shall endeavour to adopt delegated acts containing eight of the sustainability reporting standards referred to in the third subparagraph, point (ii), as soon as each is ready.
The reporting requirements laid down in the delegated acts referred to in the first subparagraph shall not enter into force earlier than four months after their adoption by the Commission.
When adopting delegated acts to specify the information required under point (ii) of the third subparagraph, the Commission shall pay particular attention to the scale of the risks and impacts related to sustainability matters for each sector, taking account of the fact that risks and impacts are higher for some sectors than for others.
The Commission shall, at least every three years after their date of application, review the delegated acts adopted pursuant to this Article, taking into consideration the technical advice of the European Financial Reporting Advisory Group (EFRAG), and, where necessary, it shall amend such delegated acts to take into account relevant developments, including developments with regard to international standards.
The Commission shall, at least once a year, consult the European Parliament, and consult jointly the Member State Expert Group on Sustainable Finance, referred to in Article 24 of Regulation (EU) 2020/852[63] and the Accounting Regulatory Committee, referred to in Article 6 of Regulation (EC) No 1606/2002,[64] on EFRAG's work program as regards the development of sustainability reporting standards.

2. The sustainability reporting standards shall ensure the quality of reported information, by requiring that it is understandable, relevant, verifiable, comparable and represented in a faithful manner. The sustainability reporting standards shall avoid imposing a disproportionate administrative burden on undertakings, including by taking account, to the greatest extent possible, of the work of global standard-setting initiatives for sustainability reporting as required by point (a) of paragraph 5.
The sustainability reporting standards shall, taking into account the subject matter of a particular sustainability reporting standard:
(a) specify the information that undertakings are to disclose about the following environmental factors:
(i) climate change mitigation, including as regards scope 1, scope 2 and, where relevant, scope 3 greenhouse gas emissions;
(ii) climate change adaptation;
(iii) water and marine resources;
(iv) resource use and the circular economy;

63 See additional text No. 17, p. 61.
64 See comment p. 107.

    (v) pollution;
    (vi) biodiversity and ecosystems;
- (b) specify the information that undertakings are to disclose about the following social and human rights factors:
    - (i) equal treatment and opportunities for all, including gender equality and equal pay for work of equal value, training and skills development, the employment and inclusion of people with disabilities, measures against violence and harassment in the workplace, and diversity;
    - (ii) working conditions, including secure employment, working time, adequate wages, social dialogue, freedom of association, existence of works councils, collective bargaining, including the proportion of workers covered by collective agreements, the information, consultation and participation rights of workers, work-life balance, and health and safety;
    - (iii) respect for the human rights, fundamental freedoms, democratic principles and standards established in the International Bill of Human Rights and other core UN human rights conventions, including the UN Convention on the Rights of Persons with Disabilities, the UN Declaration on the Rights of Indigenous Peoples, the International Labour Organization's Declaration on Fundamental Principles and Rights at Work and the fundamental conventions of the International Labour Organization, the European Convention for the protection of Human Rights and Fundamental Freedoms, the European Social Charter, and the Charter of Fundamental Rights of the European Union;
- (c) specify the information that undertakings are to disclose about the following governance factors:
    - (i) the role of the undertaking's administrative, management and supervisory bodies with regard to sustainability matters, and their composition, as well as their expertise and skills in relation to fulfilling that role or the access such bodies have to such expertise and skills;
    - (ii) the main features of the undertaking's internal control and risk management systems, in relation to the sustainability reporting and decision-making process;
    - (iii) business ethics and corporate culture, including anti-corruption and anti-bribery, the protection of whistleblowers and animal welfare;
    - (iv) activities and commitments of the undertaking related to exerting its political influence, including its lobbying activities;
    - (v) the management and quality of relationships with customers, suppliers and communities affected by the activities of the undertaking,

including payment practices, especially with regard to late payment to small and medium-sized undertakings.

3. The sustainability reporting standards shall specify the forward-looking, retrospective, qualitative and quantitative information, as appropriate, to be reported by undertakings.
4. Sustainability reporting standards shall take account of the difficulties that undertakings may encounter in gathering information from actors throughout their value chain, especially from those which are not subject to the sustainability reporting requirements laid down in Article 19a or 29a and from suppliers in emerging markets and economies. Sustainability reporting standards shall specify disclosures on value chains that are proportionate and relevant to the capacities and the characteristics of undertakings in value chains, and to the scale and complexity of their activities, especially those of undertakings that are not subject to the sustainability reporting requirements in Article 19a or 29a. Sustainability reporting standards shall not specify disclosures that would require undertakings to obtain information from small and medium-sized undertakings in their value chain that exceeds the information to be disclosed pursuant to the sustainability reporting standards for small and medium-sized undertakings referred to in Article 29c.
   The first subparagraph is without prejudice to Union requirements on undertakings to conduct a due diligence process.
5. When adopting delegated acts pursuant to paragraph 1' the Commission shall, to the greatest extent possible, take account of:
   (a) the work of global standard-setting initiatives for sustainability reporting, and existing standards and frameworks for natural capital accounting and for greenhouse gas accounting, responsible business conduct, corporate social responsibility, and sustainable development;
   (b) the information that financial market participants need in order to comply with their disclosure obligations laid down in Regulation (EU) 2019/2088 and the delegated acts adopted pursuant to that Regulation;
   (c) the criteria, indicators and methodologies set out in the delegated acts adopted pursuant to Regulation (EU) 2020/852, including the technical screening criteria established pursuant to Article 10(3),[65] Article 11(3),[66]

[65] 'Substantial contribution to climate change mitigation'; see additional text No. 18, p. 61.
[66] 'Substantial contribution to climate change adaptation'; see additional text No. 19, p. 62.

Article 12(2),[67] Article 13(2),[68] Article 14(2)[69] and Article 15(2)[70] of that Regulation and the reporting requirements set out in the delegated act adopted pursuant to Article 8 of that Regulation;[71]

(d) the disclosure requirements applicable to benchmark administrators in the benchmark statement and in the benchmark methodology and the minimum standards for the construction of EU Climate Transition Benchmarks and EU Paris-aligned Benchmarks in accordance with Commission Delegated Regulations (EU) 2020/1816,[72] (EU) 2020/1817[73] and (EU) 2020/1818;[74]

(e) the disclosures specified in the implementing acts adopted pursuant to Article 434a of Regulation (EU) No 575/2013;[75]

(f) Commission Recommendation 2013/179/EU;[76]

(g) Directive 2003/87/EC of the European Parliament and of the Council;[77]

(h) Regulation (EU) 2021/1119;[78]

(i) Regulation (EC) No 1221/2009 of the European Parliament and of the Council ;[79]

(j) Directive (EU) 2019/1937 of the European Parliament and of the Council.[80]

---

67 'Substantial contribution to the sustainable use and protection of water and marine resources'; see additional text No. 20, p. 62.

68 'Substantial contribution to the transition to a circular economy'; see additional text No. 21, p. 63.

69 'Substantial contribution to pollution prevention and control'; see additional text No. 22, p. 63.

70 'Substantial contribution to the protection and restoration of biodiversity and ecosystems'; see additional text No. 23, p. 64.

71 See additional text No. 11, p. 28.

72 ESG factors – benchmark provided and published.

73 ESG factors – benchmark methodology.

74 Minimum standards – EU Climate Transition Benchmarks and EU Paris-aligned Benchmarks; see additional text No. 24, p. 64.

75 See additional text No. 25, p. 64.

76 Product environmental footprint methodology.

77 ETS directive; see additional text No. 26, p. 65.

78 Climate neutrality regulation; see additional text No. 7, p. 25.

79 EMAS Regulation; see additional text No. 27, p. 65.

80 Whistleblower directive; see additional text No. 28, p. 66.

I. ADDITIONAL TEXTS

A. ADDITIONAL TEXT NO. 15

Commission delegated regulation (EU) 2023/2772 of 31 July 2023, European Sustainability Reporting Standards (ESRS), Annex I

European sustainability reporting standards (ESRS)

ESRS 1	General requirements
ESRS 2	General disclosures
ESRS E1	Climate change
ESRS E2	Pollution
ESRS E3	Water and marine resources
ESRS E4	Biodiversity and ecosystems
ESRS E5	Resource use and circular economy
ESRS S1	Own workforce
ESRS S2	Workers in the value chain
ESRS S3	Affected communities
ESRS S4	Consumers and end-users
ESRS G1	Business conduct

[...]

Objective

1. The objective of European Sustainability Reporting Standards (ESRS) is to specify the sustainability information that an undertaking shall disclose in accordance with Directive 2013/34/EU of the European Parliament and of the Council (1), as amended by Directive (EU) 2022/2464 of the European Parliament and of the Council. (2) Reporting in accordance with ESRS does not exempt undertakings from other obligations laid down in Union law.
2. Specifically, ESRS specify the information that an undertaking shall disclose about its material impacts, risks and opportunities in relation to environmental, social, and governance sustainability matters. ESRS do not require undertakings to disclose any information on environmental, social and governance topics covered by ESRS when the undertaking has assessed

the topic in question as non-material (See Appendix E of this Standard 'Flowchart for determining disclosures to be included').The information disclosed in accordance with ESRS enables users of the sustainability statement to understand the undertaking's material impacts on people and environment and the material effects of sustainability matters on the undertaking's development, performance and position.

3. The objective of this Standard (ESRS 1) is to provide an understanding of the architecture of ESRS, the drafting conventions and fundamental concepts used, and the general requirements for preparing and presenting sustainability information in accordance with Directive 2013/34/EU, as amended by Directive (EU) 2022/2464.

1. Categories of ESRS Standards, reporting areas and drafting conventions

1.1 Categories of ESRS standards

4. There are three categories of ESRS:
   (a) cross-cutting standards;
   (b) topical standards (Environmental, Social and Governance standards); and
   (c) sector-specific standards.

   Cross-cutting standards and topical standards are sector-agnostic, meaning that they apply to all undertakings regardless of which sector or sectors the undertaking operates in.
5. The cross-cutting standards ESRS 1 General requirements and ESRS 2 General disclosures apply to the sustainability matters covered by topical standards and sector-specific standards.
6. This standard (ESRS 1) describes the architecture of ESRS standards, explains drafting conventions and fundamental concepts, and sets out general requirements for preparing and presenting sustainability-related information.
7. ESRS 2 establishes Disclosure Requirements on the information that the undertaking shall provide at a general level across all material sustainability matters on the reporting areas governance, strategy, impact, risk and opportunity management, and metrics and targets.
8. Topical ESRS cover a sustainability topic and are structured into topics and sub-topics, and where necessary sub-sub-topics. The table in Application Requirement 16 (AR 16) to this standard provides an overview of the sustainability topics, sub-topics and sub-sub-topics (collectively 'sustainability matters') covered by topical ESRS.
9. Topical ESRS can include specific requirements that complement the general level Disclosure Requirements of ESRS 2. ESRS 2 Appendix C Disclosure/Application Requirements in topical ESRS that are applicable jointly with ESRS 2 General Disclosures provides a list of the Additional

requirements in topical ESRS that the undertaking shall apply in conjunction with the general level disclosure requirements of ESRS 2.

10. Sector-specific standards are applicable to all undertakings within a sector. They address impacts, risks and opportunities that are likely to be material for all undertakings in a specific sector and that are not covered, or not sufficiently covered, by topical standards. Sector-specific standards are multi-topical and cover the topics that are most relevant to the sector in question. Sector-specific standards achieve a high degree of comparability.
11. In addition to the disclosure requirements laid down in the three categories of ESRS, when an undertaking concludes that an impact, risk or opportunity is not covered or not covered with sufficient granularity by an ESRS but is material due to its specific facts and circumstances, it shall provide Additional entity-specific disclosures to enable users to understand the undertaking's sustainability-related impacts, risks or opportunities . Application requirements AR 1 to AR 5 provide further guidance regarding entity-specific disclosures.

1.2 Reporting areas and minimum content disclosure requirements on policies, actions, targets and metrics

12. The Disclosure Requirements in ESRS 2, in topical ESRS and in sector-specific ESRS are structured into the following reporting areas:
    (a) **Governance** (GOV): the governance processes, controls and procedures used to monitor, manage and oversee impacts, risks and opportunities (see ESRS 2, chapter 2 Governance);
    (b) **Strategy** (SBM): how the undertaking's strategy and business model interact with its material impacts, risks and opportunities, including how the undertaking addresses those impacts, risks and opportunities (see ESRS 2, chapter 3 Strategy);
    (c) **Impact**, risk and opportunity management (IRO): the process(es) by which the undertaking:
        i. identifies impacts, risks and opportunities and assesses their materiality (see IRO-1 in section 4.1 of ESRS 2),
        ii. manages material sustainability matters through policies and actions (see section 4.2 of ESRS 2).
    (d) **Metrics and targets** (MT): the undertaking's performance, including targets it has set and progress towards meeting them (see ESRS 2, chapter 5 Metrics and targets).
13. ESRS 2 includes:
    (a) in section 4.2 Minimum Disclosure Requirements regarding policies (MDR-P) and actions (MDR-A);
    (b) in section 5 Minimum Disclosure Requirements regarding metrics (MDR-M) and targets (MDR-T).

The undertaking shall apply the minimum disclosure requirements regarding policies, actions, metrics and targets together with the corresponding Disclosure Requirements in topical and sector-specific ESRS.
[...]

B. ADDITIONAL TEXT NO. 16

Regulation (EU) 2019/2088 of the European Parliament and of the Council of 27 November 2019, Sustainable Finance Disclosures Regulation (SFDR), Article 1

This Regulation lays down harmonised rules for financial market participants and financial advisers on transparency with regard to the integration of sustainability risks and the consideration of adverse sustainability impacts in their processes and the provision of sustainability-related information with respect to financial products.

C. ADDITIONAL TEXT NO. 17

Regulation (EU) 2020/852 of the European Parliament and of the Council of 18 June 2020, Taxonomy Regulation, Article 24

1. A Member State Expert Group on Sustainable Finance (the 'Member State Expert Group') shall advise the Commission on the appropriateness of the technical screening criteria and the approach taken by the Platform regarding the development of those criteria in accordance with Article 19.
2. The Commission shall inform the Member States through meetings of the Member State Expert Group to facilitate an exchange of views between the Member States and the Commission on a timely basis, in particular as regards the main output of the Platform, such as new technical screening criteria or material updates thereof, or draft reports.

D. ADDITIONAL TEXT NO. 18

Regulation (EU) 2020/852 of the European Parliament and of the Council of 18 June 2020, Taxonomy Regulation, Article 10(3)

3. The Commission shall adopt a delegated act in accordance with Article 23 to:

(a) supplement paragraphs 1 and 2 of this Article by establishing technical screening criteria for determining the conditions under which a specific economic activity qualifies as contributing substantially to climate change mitigation; and

(b) supplement Article 17 by establishing, for each relevant environmental objective, technical screening criteria for determining whether an economic activity in respect of which technical screening criteria have been established pursuant to point (a) of this paragraph causes significant harm to one or more of those objectives.

E. ADDITIONAL TEXT NO. 19

Regulation (EU) 2020/852 of the European Parliament and of the Council of 18 June 2020, Taxonomy Regulation, Article 11(3)

3. The Commission shall adopt a delegated act in accordance with Article 23 to:

(a) supplement paragraphs 1 and 2 of this Article by establishing technical screening criteria for determining the conditions under which a specific economic activity qualifies as contributing substantially to climate change adaptation; and

(b) supplement Article 17 by establishing, for each relevant environmental objective, technical screening criteria for determining whether an economic activity in respect of which technical screening criteria have been established pursuant to point (a) of this paragraph causes significant harm to one or more of those objectives.

F. ADDITIONAL TEXT NO. 20

Regulation (EU) 2020/852 of the European Parliament and of the Council of 18 June 2020, Taxonomy Regulation, Article 12(2)

2. The Commission shall adopt a delegated act in accordance with Article 23 to:

(a) supplement paragraph 1 of this Article by establishing technical screening criteria for determining the conditions under which a specific economic activity qualifies as contributing substantially to sustainable use and protection of water and marine resources; and

(b) supplement Article 17 by establishing, for each relevant environmental objective, technical screening criteria, for determining whether an economic activity in respect of which technical screening criteria have been established pursuant to point (a) of this paragraph causes significant harm to one or more of those objectives.

G. ADDITIONAL TEXT NO. 21

Regulation (EU) 2020/852 of the European Parliament and of the Council of 18 June 2020, Taxonomy Regulation, Article 13(2)

2. The Commission shall adopt a delegated act in accordance with Article 23 to:
   (a) supplement paragraph 1 of this Article by establishing technical screening criteria for determining the conditions under which a specific economic activity qualifies as contributing substantially to the transition to a circular economy; and
   (b) supplement Article 17 by establishing, for each relevant environmental objective, technical screening criteria for determining whether an economic activity in respect of which technical screening criteria have established pursuant to point (a) of this paragraph causes significant harm to one or more of those objectives.

H. ADDITIONAL TEXT NO. 22

Regulation (EU) 2020/852 of the European Parliament and of the Council of 18 June 2020, Taxonomy Regulation, Article 14(2)

2. The Commission shall adopt a delegated act in accordance with Article 23 to:
   (a) supplement paragraph 1 of this Article by establishing technical screening criteria for determining the conditions under which a specific economic activity qualifies as contributing substantially to pollution prevention and control; and
   (b) supplement Article 17 by establishing, for each relevant environmental objective, technical screening criteria for determining whether an economic activity in respect of which technical screening criteria have been established pursuant to point (a) of this paragraph causes significant harm to one or more of those objectives.

I. ADDITIONAL TEXT NO. 23

Regulation (EU) 2020/852 of the European Parliament and of the Council of 18 June 2020, Taxonomy Regulation, Article 15(2)

2. The Commission shall adopt a delegated act in accordance with Article 23 to:
   (a) supplement paragraph 1 of this Article by establishing technical screening criteria for determining the conditions under which a specific economic activity qualifies as contributing substantially to the protection and restoration of biodiversity and ecosystems; and
   (b) supplement Article 17 by establishing, for each relevant environmental objective, technical screening criteria for determining whether an economic activity in respect of which technical screening criteria have been established pursuant to point (a) of this paragraph causes significant harm to one or more of those objectives.

J. ADDITIONAL TEXT NO. 24

Commission Delegated Regulation (EU) 2020/1818 of 17 July 2020, Minimum standards – EU Climate Transition Benchmarks and EU Paris-aligned Benchmarks, Recital 3

Regulation (EU) 2016/1011 establishes EU Climate Transition Benchmarks and EU Paris-aligned Benchmarks. The methodology of those benchmarks is based on the commitments laid down in the Paris Agreement. It is necessary to specify the minimum standards applicable to both types of benchmarks. EU Climate Transition Benchmarks and EU Paris-aligned Benchmarks pursue similar objectives but vary in their level of ambition. Most of the minimum standards should therefore be common to both types of benchmarks, but the thresholds should vary depending on the type of benchmark.

K. ADDITIONAL TEXT NO. 25

Regulation (EU) No 575/2013 of the European Parliament and of the Council of 26 June 2013, Capital Requirements Regulation (CRR), Article 434a

EBA shall develop draft implementing technical standards to specify uniform disclosure formats, and information on the resubmission policy, and shall develop IT solutions, including instructions, for disclosures required under Titles II and III.

Those uniform disclosure formats shall convey sufficiently comprehensive and comparable information for users of that information to assess the risk profiles of institutions and their degree of compliance with the requirements laid down in Parts One to Seven. To facilitate the comparability of information, the implementing technical standards shall seek to maintain consistency of disclosure formats with international standards on disclosures.

Uniform disclosure formats shall be tabular where appropriate.

EBA shall submit those draft implementing technical standards to the Commission by 10 July 2025.

Power is conferred on the Commission to adopt those implementing technical standards in accordance with Article 15 of Regulation (EU) No 1093/2010.

L. ADDITIONAL TEXT NO. 26

Directive 2003/87/EC of the European Parliament and of the Council of 13 October 2003, Emission Trading Scheme (ETS) Directive, Article 1

This Directive establishes a system for greenhouse gas emission allowance trading within the Union in order to promote reductions of greenhouse gas emissions in a cost-effective and economically efficient manner.

This Directive also provides for the reductions of greenhouse gas emissions to be increased so as to contribute to the levels of reductions that are considered scientifically necessary to avoid dangerous climate change. It contributes to the achievement of the Union's climate-neutrality objective and its climate targets as laid down in Regulation (EU) 2021/1119 of the European Parliament and of the Council and thereby to the objectives of the Paris Agreement.

This Directive also lays down provisions for assessing and implementing a stricter reduction commitment exceeding 20%, to be applied upon the approval by the of an international agreement on climate change leading to greenhouse gas emission reductions exceeding those required in Article 9, as reflected in the 30% commitment endorsed by the European Council of March 2007.

M. ADDITIONAL TEXT NO. 27

Regulation (EC) No 1221/2009 of the European Parliament and of the Council of 25 November 2009, Eco-management and Audit Scheme (EMAS) Regulation, Article 1

A Community eco-management and audit scheme, hereinafter referred to as 'EMAS', is hereby established, allowing voluntary participation by organisations located inside or outside the Community.

The objective of EMAS, as an important instrument of the Sustainable Consumption and Production and Sustainable Industrial Policy Action Plan, is to promote continuous improvements in the environmental performance of organisations by the establishment and implementation of environmental management systems by organisations, the systematic, objective and periodic evaluation of the performance of such systems, the provision of information on environmental performance, an open dialogue with the public and other interested parties and the active involvement of employees in organisations and appropriate training.

N. ADDITIONAL TEXT NO. 28

Directive (EU) 2019/1937 of the European Parliament and of the Council of 23 October 2019, Whistleblower Directive, Article 1

The purpose of this Directive is to enhance the enforcement of Union law and policies in specific areas by laying down common minimum standards providing for a high level of protection of persons reporting breaches of Union law.

O. ADDITIONAL TEXT NO. 29

Directive (EU) 2024/1760 of the European Parliament and of the Council of 13 June 2024, Corporate Sustainability Due Diligence Directive (CSDDD), Article 1

1. This Directive lays down rules on:
   (a) obligations for companies regarding actual and potential human rights adverse impacts and environmental adverse impacts, with respect to their own operations, the operations of their subsidiaries, and the operations carried out by their business partners in the chains of activities of those companies;
   (b) liability for violations of the obligations as referred to in point (a); and
   (c) the obligation for companies to adopt and put into effect a transition plan for climate change mitigation which aims to ensure, through best efforts, compatibility of the business model and of the strategy of the company with the transition to a sustainable economy and with the limiting of global warming to 1,5°C in line with the Paris Agreement.
2. This Directive shall not constitute grounds for reducing the level of protection of human, employment and social rights, or of protection of the

environment or of protection of the climate provided for by the national law of the Member States or by the collective agreements applicable at the time of the adoption of this Directive.

3. This Directive shall be without prejudice to obligations in the areas of human, employment and social rights, and of protection of the environment and climate change under other Union legislative acts. If a provision of this Directive conflicts with a provision of another Union legislative act pursuing the same objectives and providing for more extensive or more specific obligations, the provision of that other Union legislative act shall prevail to the extent of the conflict and shall apply as regards those specific obligations.

II. COMMENTS

A. FIRST COMMENT

European Sustainability Standards

'Why is the Commission adopting European Sustainability Reporting Standards (ESRS)?

There is ample evidence that the sustainability information that companies currently report is not sufficient. They often omit information that investors and other stakeholders think is important. Reported information can be hard to compare from one company to another, and users of the information (such as investors) are often unsure whether they can trust it.

Problems in the quality of sustainability reporting have knock-on effects. It means that investors lack a reliable overview of sustainability-related risks to which companies are exposed. Investors increasingly should be made aware of the impact of companies on people and the environment, and their plans to reduce such impacts in the future. This knowledge will help them to meet their own disclosure requirements under the Sustainable Finance Disclosure Regulation (SFDR). More generally, if the market for green investments is to be credible, investors need to know about the sustainability impact of the companies in which they invest. Without such information, money cannot be channeled towards environmentally friendly activities.

That is why, in line with the CSRD, which outlines the obligation for companies to use standards to fulfil their legal sustainability reporting obligations, the Commission is adopting common standards which will help companies to communicate and manage their sustainability performance more efficiently, and therefore to have better access to sustainable finance.

The use of European Sustainability Reporting Standards (ESRS) will be mandatory for companies that are obliged by the Accounting Directive to report certain sustainability information. By requiring the use of common standards, the Accounting Directive, as amended by the CSRD in 2022, aims to ensure that companies across the EU report comparable and reliable sustainability information.

Common standards are expected to help companies reduce reporting costs in the medium and long term, by avoiding the use of multiple voluntary standards as is the case today. Currently, problems in the quality of sustainability reporting create an accountability gap. High-quality and reliable public reporting by companies will help create a culture of greater public accountability.

How have the ESRS been developed?

In accordance with the provisions of the Accounting Directive, as amended by the CSRD, the standards adopted by the Commission are based on technical advice (draft standards) from EFRAG. EFRAG (previously known as the European Financial Reporting Advisory Group) is an independent, multistakeholder advisory body, majority funded by the EU. Its draft standards are developed with the close involvement of investors, companies, auditors, civil society, trade unions, academics and national standard-setters.'[81]

'As part of its mandate granted by the CSRD to provide technical advice to the European Commission on European Sustainability Reporting Standards (ESRS), EFRAG is in charge of developing sector-agnostic standards, sector-specific standards, mandatory standards for listed Small and Medium Enterprises (SMEs). The development of the initial sets of ESRS will be a multi-year exercise.'[82]

'How are the ESRS structured?

There are different sets of ESRS to be used by the different companies in the CSRD's scope: the full ESRS (to be used by listed and large companies), the standard for listed SMEs, and the standard for third-country companies.

The full ESRS are made up of three categories:

- cross- cutting standards (sector-agnostic);
- topical standards (sector-agnostic); and
- sector-specific standards.

---

[81] European Commission, 'Q&A on the Adoption of European Sustainability Reporting Standards', 31 July 2023.

[82] CSRD Essentials.

- **Cross-cutting standards (ESRS 1 and ESRS 2):**
  Standards that define the general principles when reporting according to the ESRS (ESRS1). They specify the "general disclosures", which outline the essential information to be disclosed irrespective of the sustainability topics (ESRS 2) and can apply across sectors. These include: whether a company has opted to omit a specific piece of information pertaining to intellectual property, know-how or the results of innovation, or to what extent the sustainability statement covers the company's upstream and downstream value chain. ESRS 1 and ESRS 2 apply to sustainability matters described in the topical standards and sector-specific standards. The information requested by ESRS 2 is mandatory for all companies. All other standards are subject to a materiality assessment.
- **Topical standards**
  (10 of them) reflect the three dimensions of sustainable development (ESG). Each dimension is indicated by a letter and a number (for instance, ESRS S1 focuses on the social dimension, specifically on the organization and its workforce). Each topical standard is itself structured into sustainability topics, sub-topics and sub-sub-topics, collectively called "sustainability matters".'[83]
- **Sector-specific standards**
  'Sector-specific sustainability reporting standards are especially important in the case of sectors associated with high sustainability risks for or impacts on the environment, human rights and governance[84] [...]. When adopting sector-specific sustainability reporting standards, the Commission should ensure the information specified by these standards is proportionate to the scale of the risks and impacts related to sustainability matters specific to each sector, taking account of the fact that the risks and impacts of some sectors are higher than for others. The Commission should also take account of the fact that not all activities within such sectors are necessarily associated with high sustainability risks or impacts.'[85]

Following an amending decision adopted by the co-legislators, the deadline to adopt these delegated acts on sector-specific standards has been postponed by two years. Sector-specific standards should be progressively adopted, with 6 to 11 foreseen by the new deadline of June 2026. This was aimed to give more time to EFRAG to develop robust standard-setting recommendations to the European Commission.

---

83 CSRD Essentials.

84 High-risk sectors are industries that have significant environmental and social impacts due to their scale, the nature of their operations, or their resource intensity. These sectors often include energy, mining, manufacturing, agriculture, and transportation, which are associated with substantial carbon emissions, resource consumption, pollution, and social implications such as labour practices and community effects.

85 CSRD, extract from Recital 53.

B. SECOND COMMENT

Legal Interconnections with the CSRD Directive

'The EU Taxonomy Regulation on Sustainable Investment (Regulation (EU) 2020/852)

The CSRD proposes to integrate the disclosure requirements related to the EU Environmental Taxonomy into the larger framework of sustainability reporting. This means that companies falling within the scope of the CSRD would need to disclose information on the extent to which their activities are associated with environmentally sustainable economic activities, as defined by the EU Taxonomy Regulation.

The EU Taxonomy Regulation sets specific criteria for economic activities to be classified as environmentally sustainable. It focuses on economic activities that substantially contribute to one or more of the environmental objectives, without significantly harming (being detrimental) to other goals.

The environmental objectives covered by the regulation include:

- **Climate Change Mitigation**: activities that contribute to the reduction of greenhouse gas emissions and the transition to a low-carbon economy;
- **Climate Change Adaptation**: activities that enhance resilience to the impacts of climate change, helping society and ecosystems adapt to changing climate conditions;
- **Sustainable Use and Protection of Water and Marine Resources**: activities promoting the responsible and efficient use of water resources, as well as the protection and restoration of marine ecosystems;
- **Transition to a Circular Economy**: activities that contribute to the sustainable use of resources, waste prevention, and the promotion of circular business models;
- **Pollution Prevention and Control**: activities aimed at preventing pollution, reducing the release of hazardous substances, and promoting the sustainable use of resources;
- **Protection and Restoration of Biodiversity and Ecosystems**: activities that support the preservation, restoration, and sustainable use of ecosystems, biodiversity, and natural habitats.

These objectives are complemented with criteria for Sustainable Activities in each of the environmental goals mentioned above. Activities meeting these criteria can be considered as environmentally sustainable.

Article 8 of this Regulation specifically deals with the obligations of large companies and financial institutions to disclose information regarding the environmental sustainability of their economic activities, a requirement fully integrated into the CSRD.[86] Consequently, non-financial companies concerned by the CSRD are required to disclose the three ratios, namely the turnover, CapEx and OpEx in relation to economic activities which are Taxonomy-aligned. Reporting related to the Taxonomy should be incorporated into a specific section within the management report, alongside the sustainability *statement.*[87]

The Sustainable Finance Disclosures Regulation (SFDR) (Regulation (EU) 2019/2088)

The SFDR aims to enhance the transparency and sustainability of disclosures in the financial sector by establishing a framework for how financial market participants and financial advisers integrate ESG considerations into their investment processes and decision-making. It sets disclosure obligations for financial market participants, including investment firms, asset managers and insurance companies, as well as financial advisers, and for specific financial products.

To meet these obligations, financial market participants need sustainability information from companies, not only to understand the broader sustainability performance of companies covered by the CSRD, but also to better assess the sustainable nature of their investment portfolio.

The directive introduces the notion of Principal Adverse Impact (PAI). PAIs refer to the adverse effects or negative impacts that the investment decisions of financial market participants may have on ESG matters. However, the directive does not set any metrics to assess those. The ESRS should help financial institutions build relevant metrics for PAIs disclosure.

The European Climate Law (Regulation (EU) 2021/1119)

Companies in the scope of the CSRD should disclose their climate transition plan – if they have one – showing how their business model and strategy are compatible with:

- the transition to a sustainable economy;
- the limiting of global warming to 1,5 °C, in line with the Paris Agreement adopted as part of the *United Nations Framework Convention on Climate Change*; and
- the objective of carbon-neutrality (the sum between positive and negative Greenhouse Gas Emissions – GHG is net zero) of the European Climate Law.

---

86 See additional text No. 11, p. 28.

87 See comment p. 34.

This regulation establishes a legal framework in the EU to address climate change and to set the stage for achieving climate neutrality by 2050. The key elements and mandatory measures of the European Climate Law include:

- an overarching goal for the EU to become climate-neutral by 2050, with intermediate targets to reduce those by 55% by 2030 compared to 1990 levels;
- carbon budget trajectories, which allocate the total allowable emissions over a specific period for Member States;
- a governance mechanism to monitor progress, ensure accountability, and facilitate adjustments through National Energy and Climate Plans (NECPs) outlining the contributions of Member States to the EU's climate goals;
- provisions for the regular review of Member States' progress toward climate goals including an intermediate target in 2040.

EU Climate Transition Benchmarks and EU Paris-aligned Benchmarks (Delegated Regulations (EU) 2020/1816, 2020/1817, 2020/1818)

The EU Climate Transition Benchmarks and EU Paris-aligned Benchmarks are among the key legislative vehicles used by EFRAG in the development of the ESRS on climate reporting.

These benchmarks are designed to help investors identify environmentally sustainable economic activities, and investments aligned with the objectives of the Paris Agreement on climate change. They strongly connect with the EU Taxonomy Regulation: to qualify and comply with an EU Climate Transition Benchmark, companies' activities and revenues to be considered as sustainable must meet certain requirements, such as minimum carbon reduction and maximum carbon content.

Corporate Sustainability Due Diligence Directive (CSDDD) (Directive (EU) 2024/1760)

The Due Diligence Directive lays down obligations for large companies regarding actual and potential adverse impacts on the environment and human rights for their business chain of activities. This includes coverage of the upstream business partners of the company. Additionally, it partially encompasses downstream partners' activities. These activities involve distribution, transport, and storage. The directive requires companies to adopt a plan ensuring that their business model and strategy are compatible with the Paris Agreement on climate change. It also lays down rules on penalties and civil liability for infringing these obligations.

While the CSRD sets mandatory disclosure requirements for companies on their due diligence processes (obligation to tell), the CSDDD will require about 5,500 companies to identify, prevent, mitigate, communicate and remedy adverse impacts in their value chain (obligation to act). This means that companies within its scope have to describe how they act on due diligence in their management report, using the ESRS. That includes defining a climate transition plan in line with the Paris Agreement on climate change, and consistent with the objective of meeting carbon neutrality by 2050.

The directive has been formally adopted by European policymakers in April 2024.[88] Starting with EU and non-EU companies with over 5,000 employees and/or EUR 1500 million net turnover, it should progressively enter into force three years after its adoption.

Companies falling within the CSDDD scope but not covered by the CSRD, including certain sizable third-country companies operating in Europe without branches or subsidiaries, will have to communicate their due diligence obligations, taking into account certain reporting requirements included in the European Sustainability Reporting Standards, such as environmental Taxonomy-related disclosures (Regulation (EU) 2020/852, see comments pp. 34 and 70). This communication will be guided by dedicated reporting criteria, to be established at a later stage by the European Commission.'[89]

88 See additional text No. 29, p. 66.
89 CSRD Essentials.

LEGAL INTERCONNECTIONS

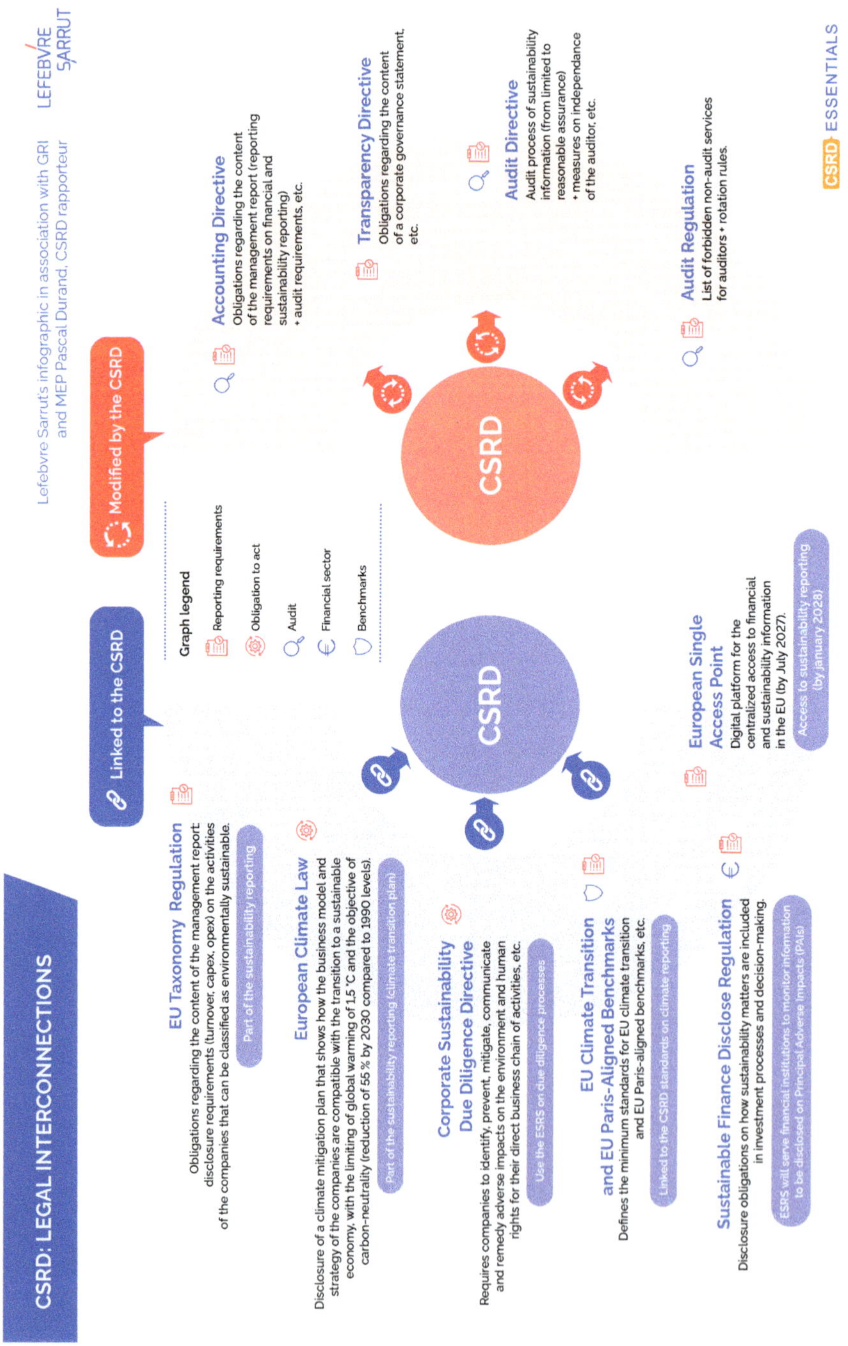

ARTICLE 29C

SUSTAINABILITY REPORTING STANDARDS FOR SMALL AND MEDIUM-SIZED UNDERTAKINGS

1. The Commission shall, by 30 June 2024, adopt delegated acts in accordance with Article 49 supplementing this Directive to provide for sustainability reporting standards proportionate and relevant to the capacities and the characteristics of small and medium-sized undertakings and to the scale and complexity of their activities. Those sustainability reporting standards shall specify for the small and medium-sized undertakings referred to in point (1)(a) of Article 2[90] the information that is to be reported in accordance with Article 19a(6).
   The reporting requirements laid down in the delegated acts referred to in the first subparagraph shall not enter into force earlier than four months after their adoption by the Commission.
2. Sustainability reporting standards for small and medium-sized undertakings shall take into account the criteria set out in Article 29b(2) to (5). They shall also, to the extent possible, specify the structure to be used to present that information.
3. The Commission shall, at least every three years after their date of application, review the delegated acts adopted pursuant to this Article, taking into consideration the technical advice of the EFRAG and, where necessary, it shall amend such delegated acts to take into account relevant developments, including developments with regard to international standards.

---

90 Public-interest entities governed by the law of a Member State and whose transferable securities are admitted to trading on a regulated market of any Member State.

COMMENTS

CSRD DIRECTIVE AND SMES

The Accounting Directive 2013/34/EU, as amended by the CSRD, imposes no new reporting requirements on SMEs, except listed SMEs.

For listed SMEs, the Accounting Directive nevertheless provides for a proportionate reporting regime. Listed SMEs are not required to report sustainability information until financial year 2026, with the possibility of an additional two-year opt-out after that. In addition, listed SMEs may report according to separate, proportionate standards that will be less demanding than the full set of ESRS that the Commission has just adopted in July 2023. EFRAG is currently developing the draft versions of the proportionate standards for listed SMEs.

Some non-listed SMEs, which are not subject to any sustainability reporting requirements under the Accounting Directive, may nevertheless receive requests for sustainability information from customers, banks, investors or other stakeholders. EFRAG is therefore also developing simpler, voluntary standards for use by non-listed SMEs. These voluntary standards should enable non-listed SMEs to respond to requests for sustainability information in an efficient and proportionate manner, and to facilitate their participation in the transition to a sustainable economy.

In addition, the CSRD Directive states that the standards for listed SMEs will legally cap the information which ESRS can require large undertakings to obtain from SMEs in their value chains. 'The sustainability reporting standards for small and medium-sized undertakings will therefore constitute a reference for undertakings that are within the scope of the requirements introduced by this amending Directive regarding the level of sustainability information that they could reasonably request from small and medium-sized undertakings that are suppliers or clients in the value chains of such undertakings.'[91]

In consideration of the European elections timing and a shifting political landscape, the sustainability reporting standards for small and medium-sized undertakings will in fact be adopted after June 2024.

[91] CSRD, extract from Recital 21.

ARTICLE 29D
SINGLE ELECTRONIC REPORTING FORMAT

1. Undertakings subject to the requirements of Article 19a of this Directive shall prepare their management report in the electronic reporting format specified in Article 3 of Commission Delegated Regulation (EU) 2019/815[92] and shall mark up their sustainability reporting, including the disclosures provided for in Article 8 of Regulation (EU) 2020/852,[93] in accordance with the electronic reporting format specified in that Delegated Regulation.
2. Parent undertakings subject to the requirements of Article 29a shall prepare their consolidated management report in the electronic reporting format specified in Article 3 of Delegated Regulation (EU) 2019/815 and shall mark up their sustainability reporting, including the disclosures provided for in Article 8 of Regulation (EU) 2020/852, in accordance with the electronic reporting format specified in that Delegated Regulation.

COMMENTS

EUROPEAN SINGLE ELECTRONIC REPORTING FORMAT (ESEF)

Since 2020, companies listed on European regulated markets should use the European Single Electronic Reporting Format (ESEF) to prepare their annual financial reports. The CSRD extends this obligation to non-listed companies which fall under the scope of the Directive. Companies will be required to structure both financial and sustainability information in a single report that is based on ESEF. In other words, companies will need to prepare their management report using the XHTML format, which is human-readable and can be opened, viewed and printed with normal web browsers. The financial and sustainability information contained in the report will require a tag on their sustainability information via a digital markup based on technical specifications system that reflect IFRS requirements for information tagging.

---

[92] ESEF Regulation; issuers shall prepare their entire annual financial reports in XHTML format.

[93] See additional text No. 11, p. 28.

The electronic semantics used is called XBRL. Online XBRL is a format that allows to embed XBRL tags in the XHTML document.

EUROPEAN SINGLE ACCESS POINT (ESAP)

'A digital taxonomy for the Union sustainability reporting standards will be necessary to allow the reported information to be tagged in accordance with these sustainability reporting standards. These requirements should feed into the work on digitalisation announced by the Commission in its Communication of 19 February 2020 entitled '"A European strategy for data" and in its Communication of 24 September 2020 entitled "Digital Finance Strategy for the EU". These requirements would also complement the creation of a European Single Access Point (ESAP) for public corporate information as envisaged in the Commission's Communication of 24 September 2020 entitled "A Capital Markets Union for people and businesses - new action plan" in which the need to provide comparable information in a digital format is also considered.'[94]

[94] CSRD, extract from Recital 55.

ARTICLE 30
GENERAL PUBLICATION REQUIREMENT

Extract

1. Member States shall ensure that undertakings publish within a reasonable period of time, which shall not exceed 12 months after the balance sheet date, the duly approved annual financial statements and the management report, in the electronic reporting format referred to in Article 29d of this Directive where applicable, together with the opinion and statement submitted by the statutory auditor or audit firm referred to in Article 34 of this Directive as laid down by the laws of each Member State in accordance with Chapter III of Title 1 of Directive (EU) 2017/1132[95] of the European Parliament and of the Council.[96]

   Member States may require undertakings subject to Articles 19a and 29a to make the management report available to the public on their website, free of charge. Where an undertaking does not have a website, Member States may require it to make a written copy of its management report available upon request.

   Where an independent assurance services provider expresses the opinion referred to in point (aa) of the second subparagraph of Article 34(1),[97] that opinion shall be published together with the documents referred to in the first subparagraph of this paragraph.

   Member States may, however, exempt undertakings from the obligation to publish the management report where a copy of all or part of any such report can be easily obtained upon request at a price not exceeding its administrative cost.

95 Company Law Directive.

96 This chapter deals with disclosure and interconnection of central, commercial and companies registers.

97 Opinion based on a limited assurance engagement as regards the compliance of the sustainability reporting with the requirements of this Directive.

The exemption laid down in the fourth subparagraph of this paragraph shall not apply to undertakings subject to the requirements on sustainability reporting laid down in Articles 19a and 29a.
[...]

COMMENTS

COMPANY LAW DIRECTIVE AND CSRD

Directive (EU) 2017/1132 focuses on the rules regarding the formation of companies in the European Union. It outlines procedures for setting up public limited liability companies (PLCs), private limited liability companies (Ltd), and other types of companies within the EU. Chapter III includes provisions related to registration procedures, and disclosure obligations for companies.

ARTICLE 33
RESPONSIBILITY AND LIABILITY FOR DRAWING UP AND PUBLISHING THE FINANCIAL STATEMENTS AND THE MANAGEMENT REPORT

1. Member States shall ensure that the members of the administrative, management and supervisory bodies of an undertaking, acting within the competences assigned to them by national law, have collective responsibility for ensuring that the following documents are drawn up and published in accordance with the requirements of this Directive and, where applicable, with the international accounting standards adopted pursuant to Regulation (EC) No 1606/2002,[98] with Delegated Regulation (EU) 2019/815,[99] with the sustainability reporting standards referred to in Article 29b or Article 29c of this Directive, and with the requirements of Article 29d of this Directive:
   (a) the annual financial statements, the management report[100] and the corporate governance statement[101] when provided separately; and
   (b) the consolidated financial statements, the consolidated management reports and the consolidated corporate governance statement when provided separately.

[2. Member States shall ensure that their laws, regulations and administrative provisions on liability, at least towards the undertaking, apply to the members of the administrative, management and supervisory bodies of the undertakings for breach of the duties referred to in paragraph 1.]

---

98 The regulation requires all listed companies in the EU to prepare their consolidated financial statements in accordance with International Financial Reporting Standards (IFRS).

99 ESEF Regulation; see comment p. 77.

100 See comment p. 17.

101 See comment p. 39.

COMMENTS

COLLECTIVE RESPONSIBILITY

'Article 33 of Directive 2013/34/EU requires Member States to ensure that the members of the administrative, management and supervisory bodies of an undertaking have collective responsibility for ensuring that the annual financial statements, the consolidated financial statements, the management report, the consolidated management report, the corporate governance statement and the consolidated corporate governance statement are drawn up and published in accordance with the requirements of that Directive. That collective responsibility should be extended to the digitalisation requirements laid down in Delegated Regulation (EU) 2019/815, to the requirement to comply with Union sustainability reporting standards, and to the requirement to mark up sustainability reporting.'[102]

[102] CSRD, Recital 59.

ARTICLE 34
GENERAL REQUIREMENT

[1. Member States shall ensure that the financial statements of public-interest entities, medium-sized and large undertakings are audited by one or more statutory auditors or audit firms approved by Member States to carry out statutory audits on the basis of Directive 2006/43/EC.

The statutory auditor(s) or audit firm(s) shall also:

(a) express an opinion on:

(i) whether the management report is consistent with the financial statements for the same financial year, and]

(ii) whether the management report has been prepared in accordance with the applicable legal requirements, excluding the requirements on sustainability reporting laid down in Article 19a of this Directive;

(aa) where applicable, express an opinion based on a limited assurance engagement as regards the compliance of the sustainability reporting with the requirements of this Directive, including the compliance of the sustainability reporting with the sustainability reporting standards adopted pursuant to Article 29b or Article 29c, the process carried out by the undertaking to identify the information reported pursuant to those sustainability reporting standards, and the compliance with the requirement to mark up sustainability reporting in accordance with Article 29d, and as regards the compliance with the reporting requirements provided for in Article 8 of Regulation (EU) 2020/852;[103]

[(b) state whether, in the light of the knowledge and understanding of the undertaking and its environment obtained in the course of the audit, he, she or it has identified material misstatements in the management report, and shall give an indication of the nature of any such misstatements.

2. The first subparagraph of paragraph 1 shall apply mutatis mutandis with respect to consolidated financial statements. The second subparagraph of paragraph 1 shall apply mutatis mutandis with respect to consolidated financial statements and consolidated management reports.]

3. Member States may allow a statutory auditor or an audit firm other than the one(s) carrying out the statutory audit of financial statements to

---

103 See additional text No. 11, p. 28.

express the opinion referred to in point (aa) of the second subparagraph of paragraph 1.

4. Member States may allow an independent assurance services provider established in their territory to express the opinion referred to in point (aa) of the second subparagraph of paragraph 1, provided that such independent assurance services provider is subject to requirements that are equivalent to those set out in Directive 2006/43/EC of the European Parliament and of the Council as regards the assurance of sustainability reporting as defined in point 22 of Article 2 of that Directive, in particular the requirements on:
   (a) training and examination, ensuring that independent assurance services providers acquire the necessary expertise concerning sustainability reporting and the assurance of sustainability reporting;
   (b) continuing education;
   (c) quality assurance systems;
   (d) professional ethics, independence, objectivity, confidentiality and professional secrecy;
   (e) appointment and dismissal;
   (f) investigations and sanctions;
   (g) the organisation of the work of the independent assurance services provider, in particular in terms of sufficient resources and personnel and the maintenance of client account records and files; and
   (h) reporting irregularities.

   Member States shall ensure that, where an independent assurance services provider expresses the opinion referred to in point (aa) of the second subparagraph of paragraph 1 of this Article, that opinion is prepared in accordance with Articles 26a, 27a and 28a of Directive 2006/43/EC and that, where applicable, the audit committee, or a dedicated committee, reviews and monitors the independence of the independent assurance services provider in accordance with point (e) of Article 39(6) of Directive 2006/43/EC.

   Member States shall ensure that independent assurance services providers accredited before 1 January 2024 for the assurance of sustainability reporting, in accordance with Regulation (EC) No 765/2008,[104] are not subject to the training and examination requirements referred to in point (a) of the first subparagraph of this paragraph.

   Member States shall ensure that independent assurance services providers that on 1 January 2024 are undergoing the accreditation process in accordance with the relevant national requirements are not subject to the training and examination requirements referred to in point (a) of the first subparagraph

[104] Setting out the requirements for accreditation and market surveillance relating to the marketing of products, see comment p. 12.

as regards the assurance of sustainability reporting, provided they complete that process by 1 January 2026.

Member States shall ensure that the independent assurance services providers referred to in the third and fourth subparagraphs acquire the necessary knowledge in sustainability reporting and the assurance of sustainability reporting via the continuing education requirement referred to in point (b) of the first subparagraph.

If a Member State, pursuant to the first subparagraph, decides to allow an independent assurance services provider to express the opinion referred to in point (aa) of the second subparagraph of paragraph 1, it shall also allow a statutory auditor other than the one(s) carrying out the statutory audit of financial statements to do so, as provided for in paragraph 3.

5. From 6 January 2027, a Member State that has made use of the option provided for in paragraph 4 (the 'host Member State') shall allow independent assurance services provider established in a Member State other than the host Member State (the 'home Member State') to carry out the assurance of sustainability reporting.

   The home Member State shall be responsible for the supervision of the independent assurance services providers established in its territory, unless the host Member State decides to supervise the assurance of sustainability reporting carried out by independent assurance services providers in its territory.

   If the host Member State decides to supervise the assurance of sustainability reporting carried out in its territory by independent assurance services providers registered in another Member State, the host Member State shall:

   (a) not impose more stringent requirements or liability on such independent assurance services providers than those required for assurance of sustainability reporting by the national laws for the independent assurance services providers or auditors established in that host Member State; and
   (b) inform other Member States about its decision to supervise the assurance of sustainability reporting carried out by independent assurance services providers established in other Member States.

6. Member States shall ensure that where an undertaking is required by Union law to have elements of its sustainability reporting verified by an accredited independent third party, the report of the accredited independent third party is made available either as an annex to the management report or by other publicly accessible means.

COMMENTS

LIMITED ASSURANCE OF THE SUSTAINABILITY REPORTING

Article 34(1) of the Directive 2013/34/EU describes the obligation for the statutory auditor(s) or audit firm(s) to express an opinion based on a limited assurance engagement on the compliance of the sustainability reporting with the European Sustainability Reporting Standards (ESRS).

It also covers the requirement for the auditor(s) to verify that the undertaking has properly identified material information and has marked it up electronically in compliance with the European Single Electronic Format (ESEF).[105]

'Statutory auditors or audit firms already verify the financial statements and the management report. The assurance of sustainability reporting by the statutory auditors or audit firms would help to ensure the connectivity between, and consistency of, financial and sustainability information, which is particularly important for users of sustainability information. However, there is a risk of further concentration of the audit market, which could risk the independence of auditors and increase audit fees or fees relating to the assurance of sustainability reporting.'[106]

INDEPENDENT ASSURANCE SERVICES PROVIDERS[107]

'Considering the key role of statutory auditors when providing assurance of sustainability reporting and ensuring reliable sustainability information, the Commission has announced that it will act to further enhance audit quality and to create a more open and diversified audit market, which are the conditions for the successful application of this amending Directive. In addition, it is desirable to offer undertakings a broader choice of independent assurance services providers for the assurance of sustainably reporting. Member States should therefore be allowed to accredit independent assurance services providers in accordance with Regulation (EC) No 765/2008 of the European Parliament and of the Council to provide an assurance opinion on sustainability reporting, which should be published together with the management report. In addition, Member States should be given the option of allowing a statutory auditor, other than the one(s) carrying out the statutory audit of the financial statements, to express an assurance opinion on sustainability reporting. Furthermore, if they

105 See comment p. 77.
106 CSRD, Recital 61.
107 See comment p. 12.

allow independent assurance services providers to carry out the assurance of sustainability reporting, Member States should also allow a statutory auditor, other than the one(s) carrying out the statutory audit of the financial statements, to express an assurance opinion on sustainability reporting.'[108]

'Independent assurance services provider' or (IASPs) designate 'a firm other than the usual auditors of financial information that is allowed by Member States to audit sustainability information. Depending on the local legal frameworks, IASPs can be sustainability specialists, certification bodies, lawyers or any other entity that received an accreditation to provide sustainability assurance'.[109]

The home Member State is responsible for supervising independent assurance services providers established within its territory, unless the host Member State opts to supervise them. If the host Member State decides to supervise, it must not impose stricter requirements or liability on such providers than those required for national providers and must inform other Member States of its decision.

---

108 CSRD, Recital 61.
109 CSRD Essentials.

ARTICLE 40A

SUSTAINABILITY REPORTS CONCERNING THIRD-COUNTRY UNDERTAKINGS

1. A Member State shall require that a subsidiary undertaking established in its territory whose ultimate parent undertaking is governed by the law of a third country publish and make accessible a sustainability report covering the information specified in points (a)(iii) to (a)(v), points (b) to (f) and, where appropriate, point (h) of Article 29a(2)[110] at the group level of that ultimate third-country parent undertaking.

   The first subparagraph shall only apply to large subsidiary undertakings and to small and medium-sized subsidiary undertakings, except micro undertakings, which are public-interest entities as defined in point (a) of point (1) of Article 2.[111]

   A Member State shall require that a branch[112] located in its territory, and which is a branch of an undertaking governed by the law of a third country, which is either not part of a group or is ultimately held by an undertaking that is formed in accordance with the law of a third country publish and make accessible a sustainability report covering the information specified in points (a)(iii) to (a)(v), points (b) to (f) and, where appropriate, point (h) of Article 29a(2), at the group level, or, if not applicable, the individual level, of the third-country undertaking.

   The rule referred to in the third subparagraph shall only apply to a branch where the third-country undertaking does not have a subsidiary undertaking as referred to in the first subparagraph, and where the branch generated a net turnover of more than EUR 40 million in the preceding financial year.

   The first and third subparagraphs shall only apply to the subsidiary undertakings or branches referred to in those subparagraphs where the

---

110 This part of Article 29a lists the sustainability information that needs to be contained in the consolidated management report.

111 They should be listed companies on regulated markets of EU Member States.

112 A branch refers to an establishment set up by a company in one EU member state but outside its main place of business. Essentially, it's like a satellite office or facility of a company operating in another country within the EU. Branches allow companies to expand their presence and conduct business in different EU countries while still being part of the same legal entity.

third-country undertaking, at its group level, or, if not applicable, the individual level, generated a net turnover of more than EUR 150 million in the Union for each of the last two consecutive financial years.
Member States may require subsidiary undertakings or branches referred to in the first and third subparagraphs to send them information about the net turnover generated in their territory and in the Union by the third-country undertakings.

2. Member States shall require that the sustainability report communicated by the subsidiary undertaking or branch as referred to in paragraph 1 is drawn up in accordance with the standards adopted pursuant to Article 40b.
By way of derogation from the first subparagraph of this paragraph, the sustainability report referred to in paragraph 1 of this Article may be drawn up in accordance with the sustainability reporting standards adopted pursuant to Article 29b or in a manner equivalent to those sustainability reporting standards, as determined in accordance with an implementing act on the equivalence of sustainability reporting standards adopted pursuant to the third subparagraph of Article 23(4) of Directive 2004/109/EC.
Where the information required to draw up the sustainability report referred to in the first subparagraph of this paragraph is not available, the subsidiary undertaking or branch referred to in paragraph 1 shall request the third-country undertaking to provide them with all information necessary to enable them to meet their obligations.
In the event that not all the required information is provided, the subsidiary undertaking or branch referred to in paragraph 1 shall draw up, publish and make accessible the sustainability report referred to in paragraph 1, containing all information in its possession, obtained or acquired, and issue a statement indicating that the third-country undertaking did not make the necessary information available.
3. Member States shall require that the sustainability report referred to in paragraph 1 is published accompanied by an assurance opinion expressed by one or more person(s) or firm(s) authorized to give an opinion on the assurance of sustainability reporting under the national law of the third-country undertaking or of a Member State.
In the event that the third-country undertaking does not provide the assurance opinion in accordance with the first subparagraph, the subsidiary undertaking or branch shall issue a statement indicating that the third-country undertaking did not make the necessary assurance opinion available.
4. Member States may inform the Commission on an annual basis of the subsidiary undertakings or branches of third-country undertakings that fulfilled the publication requirement laid down in Article 40d and of the cases where a report was published but where the subsidiary undertaking or branch has acted in accordance with the fourth subparagraph of paragraph 2

of this Article. The Commission shall make publicly available on its website a list of the third-country undertakings that publish a sustainability report.

COMMENTS

CONSOLIDATION ROUTE OF A THIRD-COUNTRY COMPANY

'Third-country undertakings which have a significant activity on the territory of the Union should also be required to provide sustainability information, especially on their impacts on social and environmental matters, in order to ensure that third-country undertakings are accountable for their impacts on people and the environment and that there is a level playing field for companies operating in the internal market. Therefore, third-country undertakings which generate a net turnover of more than EUR 150 million in the Union and which have a subsidiary undertaking or a branch on the territory of the Union should be subject to Union sustainability reporting requirements.

To ensure the proportionality and enforceability of such requirements, the threshold of having a net turnover of more than EUR 40 million should apply to the branches of third-country undertakings, and the thresholds related to being considered a large undertaking or a small or medium-sized undertaking, except micro undertakings, whose securities are admitted to trading on a regulated market in the Union should apply to the subsidiary undertakings of third-country undertakings, as such subsidiary undertakings and branches should be responsible for publishing the sustainability report of the third-country undertaking.

The subsidiary undertaking or branch of a third-country undertaking should also be able to report in accordance with the standards applying to undertakings established in the Union, or in accordance with standards which are deemed equivalent pursuant to an implementing act. In the event that not all the information required under this amending Directive is provided by the third-country undertaking, despite the best efforts of the subsidiary undertaking or branch of that third-country undertaking to obtain the necessary information, that subsidiary undertaking or branch should provide all the information in its possession and issue a statement indicating that the third-country undertaking did not make the rest of the required information available. In order to ensure the quality and reliability of the reporting, the sustainability reports of third-country undertakings should be published accompanied by an assurance opinion expressed by a person or firm authorised to give an opinion on the assurance of sustainability reporting, either under the national law of the third-country undertaking or of a Member State. In the event that such an assurance opinion is not provided, the subsidiary undertaking or branch of the third-country undertaking should issue a statement indicating that the third-country undertaking did not provide the necessary assurance opinion. The sustainability report should be made accessible free of charge to the public through the central, commercial or companies registers of the Member States, or alternatively on the website of the subsidiary undertaking or the branch of the third-country undertaking.

Member States should be able to inform the Commission on an annual basis of the subsidiary undertakings or branches of the third-country undertakings that fulfilled the publication requirement and of the cases where a report was published but the subsidiary undertaking or branch of the third-country undertaking has stated that it could not get the necessary information from the third-country undertaking. The Commission should make publicly available on its website a list of the third-country undertakings that have published a sustainability report.'[113]

By April 2029, the Commission should provide an assessment of the implementation of the reporting requirements for subsidiaries and branches of third-country, including an assessment of the number of third-country companies.

WHICH STANDARDS SHOULD BE USED?

Third-country companies meeting the above-mentioned conditions have the following options for reporting their sustainability information, from fiscal year 2028 onwards:

- use the standards for third-country companies;
- use the full sets of ESRS available to date; and
- use their own domestic reporting rules (for them, exclusively on impact materiality), provided that applicable standards set by those rules are deemed equivalent to the ESRS by the European Commission.

The same applies to parent companies outside the EU that want to consolidate the reporting of their EU subsidiaries. The European Commission assesses the equivalence on a country-by-country basis, following a request by a country to do so.

While the CSRD provides the European Commission with the possibility to allow in-scope third-country companies to use sustainability standards equivalent to the ESRS, it has not yet decided which standards would be deemed equivalent.

[113] CSRD, Recital 20.

CONSOLIDATION OF A THIRD-COUNTRY PARENT GROUP WITH SUBSIDIARIES OR BRANCHES IN THE EU

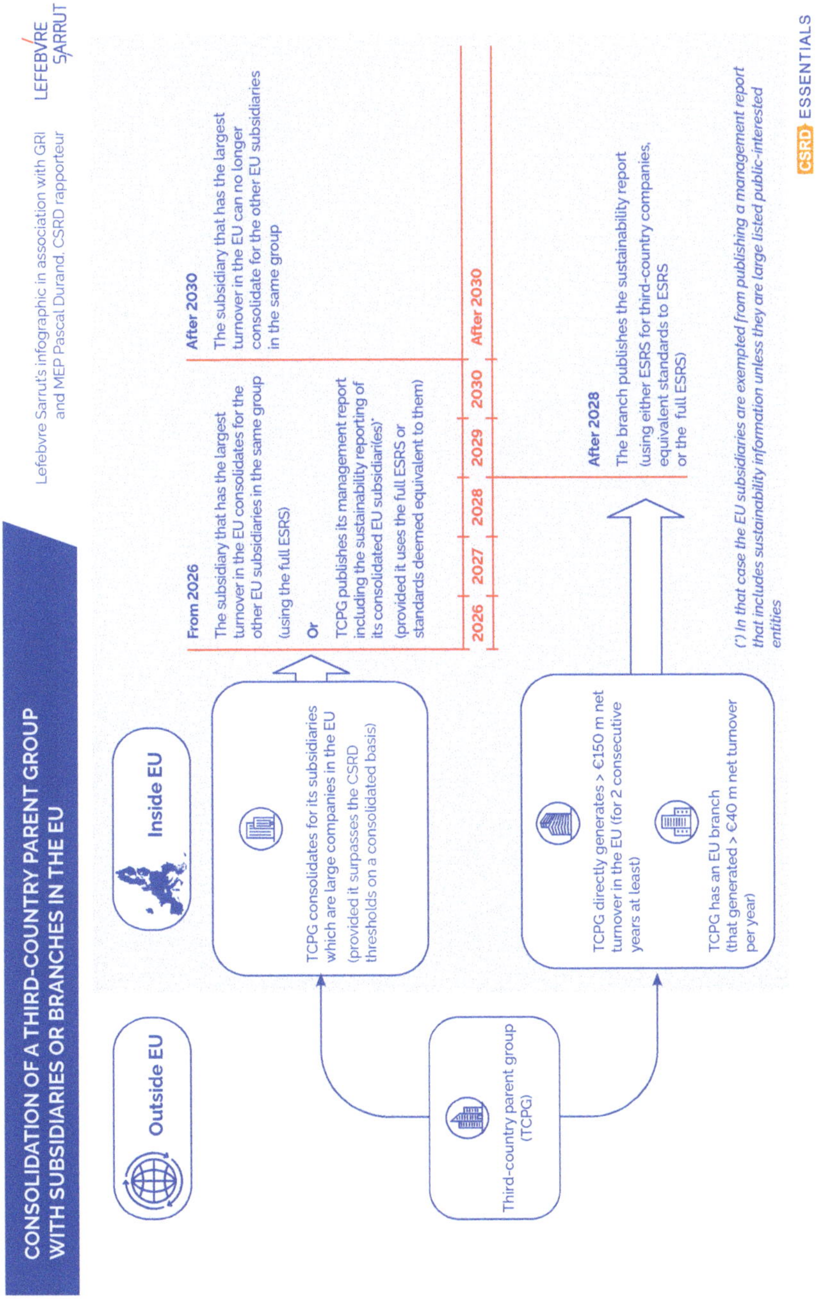

CONSOLIDATION OF A THIRD-COUNTRY PARENT COMPANY THAT HAS LISTED SUBSIDIARIES IN THE EU

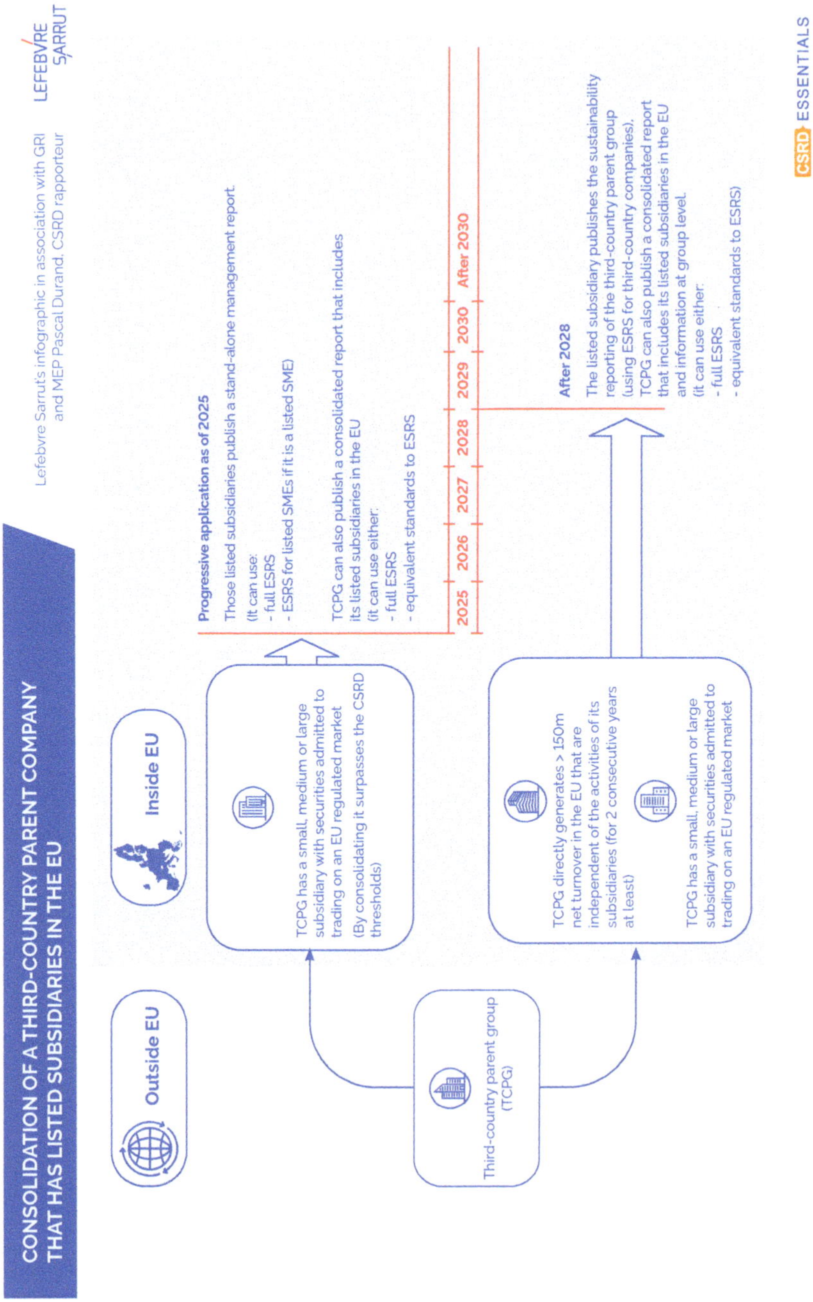

ARTICLE 40B

SUSTAINABILITY REPORTING STANDARDS FOR THIRD-COUNTRY UNDERTAKINGS

The Commission shall adopt by 30 June 2026[114] a delegated act in accordance with Article 49 supplementing this Directive to provide for sustainability reporting standards for third-country undertakings that specify the information that is to be included in the sustainability reports referred to in Article 40a.

COMMENTS

POSTPONING OF ESRS FOR NON-EU COMPANIES

The sustainability reports published by the subsidiary undertaking or branch of a third-country undertaking should be prepared in accordance with standards for third-country companies to be adopted by 30 June 2026 by the Commission through delegated acts, following a decision to postpone the initial adoption date by two years.[115]

---

114 It has been postponed from 30 June 2024 to 30 June 2026.

115 Directive (EU) 2024/1306 of the European Parliament and of the Council of 29 April 2024; see comment p. 67.

ARTICLE 40C

RESPONSIBILITY FOR DRAWING UP, PUBLISHING AND MAKING ACCESSIBLE SUSTAINABILITY REPORTS CONCERNING THIRD-COUNTRY UNDERTAKINGS

Member States shall provide that the branches[116] of third-country undertakings are responsible for ensuring, to the best of their knowledge and ability, that their sustainability report is drawn up in accordance with Article 40a and that report is published and made accessible in accordance with Article 40d.

Member States shall provide that the members of the administrative, management and supervisory bodies of the subsidiary undertakings referred to in Article 40a have collective responsibility for ensuring, to the best of their knowledge and ability, that their sustainability report is drawn up in accordance with Article 40a, and that that report is published and made accessible in accordance with Article 40d.

---

[116] See comment p. 91, n. 112.

ARTICLE 40D
PUBLICATION

1. The subsidiary undertakings and branches referred to in Article 40a(1) of this Directive shall publish their sustainability report, together with the assurance opinion and, where applicable, the statement mentioned in the fourth subparagraph of Article 40a(2) of this Directive, within 12 months of the balance sheet date of the financial year for which the report is drawn up, as provided for by each Member State, in accordance with Articles 14 to 28 of Directive (EU) 2017/1132[117] and, where relevant, in accordance with Article 36[118] of that Directive.
2. Where the sustainability report together with the assurance opinion and, where applicable, with the statement published in accordance with paragraph 1 of this Article, are not made accessible, free of charge, to the public on the website of the register referred to in Article 16[119] of Directive (EU) 2017/1132, Member States shall ensure that the sustainability report together with the assurance opinion and, where applicable, with the statement published by the undertakings in accordance with paragraph 1 of this Article, are made accessible to the public in at least one of the official languages of the Union, free of charge, no later than 12 months after the balance sheet date of the financial year for which the report is drawn up, on the website of the subsidiary undertaking or the branch as referred to in Article 40a(1) of this Directive.

COMMENTS

REPORTING BY THIRD-COUNTRY COMPANIES AND NATIONAL REGISTERS[120]

The sustainability report published by the branches and subsidiaries of companies with headquarters outside the EU should be made accessible free of

[117] Company Law Directive.
[118] 'Disclosure of documents and particulars relating to a branch'.
[119] 'Disclosure in the register'.
[120] See comment p. 80.

charge to the public through the central, commercial or companies registers of the Member States, or alternatively on the website of the subsidiary undertaking or the branch of the third-country undertaking.

In connection with Article 40d, Articles 14 to 28 of Directive (EU) 2017/1132, often referred to as the Company Law Directive, are relevant as they lay the foundation for the organisation and functioning of national registers of companies. These articles cover a range of requirements, including the disclosure of company information, the maintenance of accurate and up-to-date records, and the interoperability of registers across the EU. The Company Law Directive mandates that Member States ensure the availability of certain minimum information about companies in a central, commercial, or companies register. This information includes details about the company's legal form, its registered office, its articles of association, and the identities of its directors.

The Company Law Directive's provisions on national registers are crucial for ensuring the effectiveness of financial transparency measures as outlined in this article. The national registers also serve as repositories for the publicly disclosed information mandated by this article.

ARTICLE 48I
TRANSITIONAL PROVISIONS

1. Until 6 January 2030, Member States shall permit a Union subsidiary undertaking which is subject to Article 19a or 29a and whose parent undertaking is not governed by the law of a Member State to prepare consolidated sustainability reporting, in accordance with the requirements of Article 29a, that includes all Union subsidiary undertakings of such parent undertaking that are subject to Article 19a or 29a.
   Until 6 January 2030, Member States shall permit the consolidated sustainability reporting referred to in the first subparagraph of this paragraph to include the disclosures laid down in Article 8 of Regulation (EU) 2020/852[121] *covering* the activities carried out by all Union subsidiary undertakings of the parent undertaking referred to in the first subparagraph of this paragraph that are subject to Article 19a or 29a of this Directive.
2. The Union subsidiary undertaking referred to in paragraph 1 shall be one of the Union subsidiary undertakings of the group that generated the greatest turnover in the Union in at least one of the preceding five financial years, on a consolidated basis where applicable.
3. The consolidated sustainability reporting referred to in paragraph 1 of this Article shall be published in accordance with Article 30.
4. For the purpose of the exemption laid down in Article 19a(9)[122] and Article 29a(8),[123] reporting in accordance with paragraph 1 of this Article shall be considered to be reporting by a parent undertaking at group level with respect to the undertakings included in the consolidation. Reporting in accordance with the second subparagraph of paragraph 1 of this Article shall be considered to fulfill the conditions referred to in point (c) of the second subparagraph of Article19a(9) and point (c) of the second subparagraph of Article 29a(8), respectively.

---

[121] See additional text No. 11, p. 28.

[122] Exemption for subsidiary undertakings.

[123] Exemption to include in the stand-alone management report information necessary to understand the undertaking's impacts on sustainability matters, and information necessary to understand how sustainability matters affect the undertaking's development, performance and position in case those are included in the consolidated management report of another parent undertaking.

COMMENTS

THE SPECIFIC CASE OF SUBSIDIARIES WITH PARENT COMPANIES BASED OUTSIDE THE EU

'A distinctive form of the subsidiary exemption is currently applicable (on a temporary basis) to EU subsidiaries or subgroups, with a parent company headquartered outside the EU. Until 2030, these companies may be exempted from individual reporting requirements if they are incorporated into a report using ESRS and "artificial consolidation", meaning that the EU subsidiaries and subgroups are consolidated. The entity responsible for consolidating other EU-based subsidiaries is the one with the highest turnover within the EU. The purpose of this transitional provision is to reduce the burden for the non-EU groups that do not have a single EU-based holding entity that controls the group's EU entities.

The ultimate parent companies that are not based in the EU may also consolidate their EU subsidiaries in a global sustainability statement. However, such consolidation exempts the EU subsidiaries from the obligation to produce their own sustainability statements only if the global consolidated statement is drawn up in accordance with the ESRS, or in an equivalent manner.'[124]

[124] CSRD Essentials; see comment p. 91.

ARTICLE 49
EXERCISE OF DELEGATED POWERS

Extract

[1. The power to adopt delegated acts is conferred on the Commission subject to the conditions laid down in this Article.]

2. The power to adopt delegated acts referred to in Article 1(2),[125] Article 3(13),[126] Articles 29b, 29c and 40b, and Article 46(2)[127] shall be conferred on the Commission for a period of 5 years from 5 January 2023. The Commission shall draw up a report in respect of the delegation of power not later than nine months before the end of the 5-year period. The delegation of power shall be tacitly extended for periods of an identical duration, unless the European Parliament or the Council opposes such extension not later than three months before the end of each period.
3. The delegation of power referred to in Article 1(2), Article 3(13), Articles 29b, 29c and 40b, and Article 46(2) may be revoked at any time by the European Parliament or by the Council. A decision to revoke shall put an end to the delegation of the power specified in that decision. It shall take effect the day following the publication of that decision in the Official Journal of the European Union or at a later date specified therein. It shall not affect the validity of any delegated acts already in force.

[...]

---

125 Art. 1(2): 'Member States shall inform the Commission within a reasonable period of time of changes in the types of undertakings in their national law that may affect the accuracy of Annex I or Annex II. In such a case, the Commission shall be empowered to adapt, by means of delegated acts in accordance with Article 49, the lists of undertakings contained in Annexes I and II.'; see additional texts No. 2, p. 5, and No. 30, p. 105.

126 Art. 3(13): 'In order to adjust for the effects of inflation, the Commission shall at least every five years review and, where appropriate, amend, by means of delegated acts in accordance with Article 49, the thresholds referred to in paragraphs 1 to 7 of this Article, taking into account measures of inflation as published in the Official Journal of the European Union.'

127 Art. 46(2): 'The Commission shall be empowered to adopt delegated acts identifying the criteria to be applied when assessing the equivalence of third-country reporting requirements and the requirements of a chapter of directive 2013/34/EU which deals with report on payments to governments.'

3b. When adopting delegated acts pursuant to Articles 29b and 29c, the Commission shall take into consideration technical advice from EFRAG, provided that:

(a) such advice has been developed with proper due process, public oversight and transparency, with the expertise and balanced participation of relevant stakeholders, and with sufficient public funding to ensure its independence, and on the basis of a work programme on which the Commission has been consulted;

(b) such advice is accompanied by cost-benefit analyses that include analyses of the impacts of the technical advice on sustainability matters;

(c) such advice is accompanied by an explanation of how it takes account of the elements listed in Article 29b (5);

(d) participation in EFRAG's work at technical level is based on expertise in sustainability reporting and is not conditional on a financial contribution.

Points (a) and (d) are without prejudice to the participation of public bodies and national standard-setting organizations in the technical work of EFRAG.

The accompanying documents for the EFRAG technical advice shall be submitted together with that technical advice.

The Commission shall consult jointly the Member State Expert Group on Sustainable Finance, referred to in Article 24 of Regulation (EU) 2020/852,[128] and the Accounting Regulatory Committee, referred to in Article 6 of Regulation (EC) No 1606/2002,[129] on the draft delegated acts prior to their adoption as referred to in Articles 29b and 29c of this Directive.

The Commission shall request the opinion of the European Securities and Markets Authority (ESMA), the European Banking Authority (EBA) and the European Insurance and Occupational Pensions Authority (EIOPA) on the technical advice provided by EFRAG, in particular with regard to its consistency with Regulation (EU) 2019/2088,[130] and the delegated acts adopted pursuant to that Regulation. ESMA, EBA and EIOPA shall provide their opinions within two months of the date of receipt of the request from the Commission.

The Commission shall also consult the European Environment Agency, the European Union Agency for Fundamental Rights, the European Central Bank, the Committee of European Auditing Oversight Bodies and the Platform on Sustainable Finance established pursuant to Article 20 of Regulation (EU) 2020/852 on the technical advice provided by EFRAG prior to the adoption of delegated acts referred to in Articles 29b and 29c of this Directive. If any of those bodies decide to submit an opinion, they shall do so within two months of the date of being consulted by the Commission.

---

128 See additional text No. 17, p. 61 and comment p. 34.

129 Application of international accounting standards.

130 See comment p. 71 and additionnal text No. 16, p. 61.

[...]

5. A delegated act adopted pursuant to Article 1(2), Article 3(13), Articles 29b, 29c or 40b, or Article 46(2) shall enter into force only if no objection has been expressed either by the European Parliament or the Council within a period of two months of notification of that act to the European Parliament and the Council or if, before the expiry of that period, the European Parliament and the Council have both informed the Commission that they will not object. That period shall be extended by two months at the initiative of the European Parliament or the Council.

I. ADDITIONAL TEXTS

ADDITIONAL TEXT NO. 30

Directive 2013/34/EU of the European Parliament and of the Council of 26 June 2013, Accounting Directive, Annex II

TYPES OF UNDERTAKING REFERRED TO IN POINT (b) OF ARTICLE 1(1)

- Belgium: la société en nom collectif/de vennootschap onder firma, la société en commandite simple/de gewone commanditaire vennootschap, la société coopérative à responsabilité illimitée/de coöperatieve vennootschap met onbeperkte aansprakelijkheid;
- Bulgaria: събирателно дружество, командитно дружество;
- the Czech Republic: veřejná obchodní společnost, komanditní společnost;
- Denmark: interessentskaber, kommanditselskaber;
- Germany: die offene Handelsgesellschaft, die Kommanditgesellschaft;
- Estonia: täisühing, usaldusühing;
- Ireland: partnerships, limited partnerships, unlimited companies;
- Greece: η ομόρρυθμος εταιρία, η ετερόρρυθμος εταιρία;
- Spain: sociedad colectiva, sociedad en comandita simple;
- France: la société en nom collectif, la société en commandite simple;
- In Croatia: javno trgovačko društvo, komanditno društvo, gospodarsko interesno udruženje;
- Italy: la società in nome collettivo, la società in accomandita semplice;
- Cyprus: Ομόρρυθμες και ετερόρρυθμες εταιρείες (συνεταιρισμοί);
- Latvia: pilnsabiedrība, komandītsabiedrība;
- Lithuania: tikrosios ūkinės bendrijos, komanditinės ūkinės bendrijos;
- Luxembourg: la société en nom collectif, la société en commandite simple;
- Hungary: közkereseti társaság, betéti társaság, közös vállalat, egyesülés, egyéni cég;

- Malta: soċjeta f'isem kollettiv jew soċjeta in akkomandita, bil-kapital li mhux maqsum f'azzjonijiet meta s-soċji kollha li għandhom responsabbilita' llimitata huma soċjetajiet in akkomandita bil-kapital maqsum f'azzjonijiet — partnership en nom collectif or partnership en commandite with capital that is not divided into shares, when all the partners with unlimited liability are partnership en commandite with the capital divided into shares;
- the Netherlands: de vennootschap onder firma, de commanditaire vennootschap;
- Austria: die offene Gesellschaft, die Kommanditgesellschaft;
- Poland: spółka jawna, spółka komandytowa;
- Portugal: sociedade em nome colectivo, sociedade em comandita simples;
- Romania: societate în nume colectiv, societate în comandită simplă;
- Slovenia: družba z neomejeno odgovornostjo, komanditna družba;
- Slovakia: verejná obchodná spoločnosť, komanditná spoločnosť;
- Finland: avoin yhtiö/ öppet bolag, kommandiittiyhtiö/kommanditbolag;
- Sweden: handelsbolag, kommanditbolag;
- the United Kingdom: partnerships, limited partnerships, unlimited companies.

II. COMMENTS

COMITOLOGY PROCEDURE AND THE DELEGATION OF POWER TO THE COMMISSION

'In the context of EU law, the delegation of power refers to the authority granted by the EU legislator (usually the European Parliament and the Council of the EU) to the European Commission to adopt legal acts in specific policy areas. This delegation is outlined in primary legislation and allows the Commission to supplement or amend non-essential elements of the legislation. However, this delegation comes with clear limits and conditions to ensure accountability and transparency, and the Commission must act within the framework set by the legislator.'[131]

These acts can be compared to a 'European decree', and the European Commission is empowered to adopt them under different rules of control by the Council of the EU and the European Parliament. This procedure is known as 'comitology' and is described in the Interinstitutional Agreement between the European Parliament, the Council of the EU and the European Commission on better law-making.

[131] CSRD Essentials.

SIZE THRESHOLDS FOR EU-BASED COMPANIES

Since 2013, the size thresholds of the Accounting Directive based on a company's turnover had remained unchanged. The size criteria have now been adjusted by 25% and the adjustments took the form of Commission Delegated Directive (EU) 2023/2775, which was adopted on 17 October 2023, published on 21 December 2023, and entered into force on 24 December 2023.

ROLE OF THE ACCOUNTING REGULATORY COMMITTEES AND THE MEMBER STATE EXPERT GROUP ON SUSTAINABLE FINANCE

In the exercise of these delegated powers, the European Commission can be helped by the Member State Expert Group on Sustainable Finance[132] or the Accounting Regulatory Committee. This committee assists the Commission in adopting technical implementing measures necessary for ensuring consistent and high-quality financial reporting across the European Union. It provides expertise and advice on accounting standards and practices, helping to harmonise financial reporting requirements and enhance transparency in financial markets. Overall, the committee supports the Commission in achieving the objectives of Regulation (EC) No 1606/2002[133] by promoting confidence in financial statements and facilitating cross-border investment within the EU.

Specifically, the Accounting Regulatory Committee helps the Commission to standardise financial accounting standards for publicly traded companies governed by the law of a Member State which, under certain conditions, are to prepare their consolidated accounts in conformity with international accounting standards, such as the IFRS.

ROLE OF THE PLATFORM ON SUSTAINABLE FINANCE

As part of its duties, the European Commission can also consult the 'Platform on Sustainable Finance', an advisory body established under Article 20 of the Taxonomy Regulation and subject to the Commission's horizontal rules for expert groups. Its main purpose is to advise the European Commission on the implementation and usability of the EU taxonomy and the sustainable finance

[132] See comment p. 35.
[133] Application of international accounting standards.

framework more broadly. The Platform will also work on the development and possible revisions of taxonomy criteria and on monitoring of capital flows.

Members and observers of the platform are working in three main directions to develop key deliverables:

- advising on the usability of the EU taxonomy and wider sustainable finance framework;
- advising on the technical screening criteria for the EU taxonomy; and
- monitoring capital flows into sustainable investments.

PART II

Amendments to Directive 2004/109/EC

ARTICLE 2
DEFINITIONS

Extract

[...]

1. [...]
   (d) 'issuer' means a natural person, or a legal entity governed by private or public law, including a State, whose securities are admitted to trading on a regulated market.
   In the case of depository receipts admitted to trading on a regulated market, the issuer means the issuer of the securities represented, whether or not those securities are admitted to trading on a regulated market;
   [...]
   (r) 'sustainability reporting' means sustainability reporting as defined in point (18) of Article 2 of Directive 2013/34/EU of the European Parliament and of the Council.
   [...]

ARTICLE 4
ANNUAL FINANCIAL REPORT
Extract

[...]

2. [...]
   (c) statements made by the persons responsible within the issuer, whose names and functions shall be clearly indicated, to the effect that, to the best of their knowledge, the financial statements prepared in accordance with the applicable set of accounting standards give a true and fair view of the assets, liabilities, financial position and profit or loss of the issuer and the undertakings included in the consolidation taken as a whole and that the management report includes a fair review of the development and performance of the business and the position of the issuer and the undertakings included in the consolidation taken as a whole, together with a description of the principal risks and uncertainties that they face and, where appropriate, that it is prepared in accordance with sustainability reporting standards referred to in Article 29b of Directive 2013/34/EU and with the specifications adopted pursuant to Article 8(4)[134] of Regulation (EU) 2020/852[135] of the European Parliament and of the Council.

[...]

4. The financial statements shall be audited in accordance with the first subparagraph of Article 34(1)[136] and Article 34(2) of Directive 2013/34/EU. The statutory auditor shall deliver the opinion and statement on the management report referred to in points (a) and (b) of the second subparagraph of Article 34(1) and in Article 34(2) of Directive 2013/34/EU.

---

134 Technical screening criteria; see additional text No. 11, p. 28.

135 See comments p. 34 and p. 70.

136 It sets out the general requirement for the statutory audit of financial statements of undertakings. It is amended to provide for the assurance (audit) of sustainability reporting established by undertakings.

The audit report, referred to in Article 28 of Directive 2006/43/EC of the European Parliament and of the Council, signed by the person or persons responsible for carrying out the work set out in Article 34(1) and (2) of Directive 2013/34/EU shall be disclosed in full to the public together with the annual financial report.
Where applicable, an assurance opinion on sustainability reporting shall be provided in accordance with point (aa) of the second subparagraph of Article 34(1) and Article 34(2) to (5) of Directive 2013/34/EU.
The assurance report on sustainability reporting referred to in Article 28a of Directive 2006/43/EC shall be disclosed in full to the public together with the annual financial report.

5. The management report shall be drawn up in accordance with Articles 19, 19a and 20, and Article 29d(1) of Directive 2013/34/EU, and shall include the specifications adopted pursuant to Article 8(4) of Regulation (EU) 2020/852, when drawn up by undertakings referred to in those provisions. Where the issuer is required to prepare consolidated accounts, the consolidated management report shall be drawn up in accordance with Articles 29[137] and 29a and Article 29d(2) of Directive 2013/34/EU and shall include the specifications adopted pursuant to Article 8(4) of Regulation (EU) 2020/852, when drawn up by undertakings referred to in those provisions.

COMMENTS

TRANSPARENCY DIRECTIVE AND CSRD DIRECTIVE

The Transparency Directive (2004/109/EC) aims to improve the transparency of financial markets by establishing disclosure requirements for issuers of securities listed on regulated markets. The CSRD amends this directive to ensure that companies listed on an EU regulated market adhere to the same sustainability reporting requirements as non-listed companies that fall in the scope of the Accounting Directive (*e.g.* in terms of the assurance of the sustainability information).

---

137 See additional text No. 10, p. 27; see comments pp. 17, 32 and 50.

ARTICLE 23
THIRD COUNTRIES
Extract

[...]

[4. In order to ensure the uniform conditions of application of paragraph 1, the Commission shall, in accordance with the procedure referred to in Article 27(2),[138] adopt implementing measures:

(i) setting up a mechanism ensuring the establishment of equivalence of information required under this Directive, including financial statements and information, required under the law, regulations or administrative provisions of a third country;

(ii) stating that, by reason of its domestic law, regulations, administrative provisions, or of the practices or procedures based on the international standards set by international organizations, the third country where the issuer is registered ensures the equivalence of the information requirements provided for in this Directive.

In the context of point (ii) of the first subparagraph, the Commission shall also adopt, by means of delegated acts in accordance with Article 27(2a), (2b) and (2c), and subject to the conditions of Articles 27a[139] and 27b,[140] measures concerning the assessment of standards relevant to the issuers of more than one country.]

The Commission shall, in accordance with the procedure referred to in Article 27(2) of this Directive, take the necessary decisions on the equivalence of accounting standards under the conditions set out in Article 30(3)[141] of this Directive and on the equivalence of sustainability reporting standards as referred to in Article 29b of Directive 2013/34/EU which are used by third-country issuers. If the Commission decides that the accounting standards or

[138] 'Committee procedure'.

[139] 'Revocation of the delegation'.

[140] 'Objections to delegated acts'.

[141] 'Transitional provisions'; this sub-paragraph lays down the conditions for a Member State to exempt certain listed issuers incorporated in a third country from drawing up financial statements and their management report.

the sustainability reporting standards of a third country are not equivalent, it may allow the issuers concerned to continue using such standards during an appropriate transitional period.

In the context of the third subparagraph of this paragraph, the Commission shall also adopt, by means of delegated acts adopted in accordance with Article 27(2a), (2b) and (2c), and subject to the conditions laid down in Articles 27a and 27b, measures that aim to establish general equivalence criteria regarding accounting standards and sustainability reporting standards relevant to issuers of more than one country.

The criteria that the Commission shall use when assessing the equivalence of sustainability reporting standards used by third-country issuers referred to in the third subparagraph shall at least ensure the following:

(a) that the sustainability reporting standards require undertakings to disclose information on environmental, social and governance factors;

(b) that the sustainability reporting standards require undertakings to disclose information necessary to understand their impacts on sustainability matters, and information necessary to understand how sustainability matters affect their development, performance and position.

[...]

COMMENTS

SETTING UP A MECHANISM FOR THE ESTABLISHMENT OF EQUIVALENCE OF SUSTAINABILITY INFORMATION

'[The Transparency Directive (Directive 2004/109/EC)] empowers the Commission to adopt measures to set up a mechanism for the determination of equivalence of information required under that Directive, and for the establishment of general equivalence criteria regarding accounting standards, respectively. The third subparagraph of Article 23(4) of Directive 2004/109/EC also empowers the Commission to take the necessary decisions on the equivalence of accounting standards which are used by third-country issuers. In order to reflect the inclusion of the sustainability requirements in Directive 2004/109/EC, the Commission should be empowered to establish a mechanism for the determination of equivalence of sustainability reporting standards applied by third-country issuers, similar to what is provided for in Commission Regulation (EC) No 1569/2007[142] which sets out the criteria for the determination of equivalence of accounting standards applied by

142 Mechanism for the determination of equivalence of accounting standards applied by third country issuers of securities.

third-country issuers. For the same reason, the Commission should also be empowered to take the necessary decisions on the equivalence of sustainability reporting standards that are used by third-country issuers. The amendments introduced by this amending Directive[143] will ensure consistent equivalence regimes for sustainability reporting requirements and for financial reporting requirements regarding the annual financial report.'[144]

'Undertakings whose securities are admitted to trading on a regulated market in the Union and undertakings whose securities are not admitted to trading on a regulated market in the Union should be required to report in accordance with the same sustainability reporting standards. In this context, the implementing acts adopted by the Commission pursuant to point (i) of the first subparagraph of Article 23(4) and the fourth subparagraph of Article 23(4) of Directive 2004/109/EC establishing a mechanism for the determination of equivalence of standards should be used to determine whether to exempt subsidiary undertakings of third-country parent undertakings under the regime of Directive 2013/34/EU. Such exemption should not apply to large undertakings whose securities are admitted to trading on a regulated market in the Union for reasons of investor protection, in order to ensure greater transparency as regards such undertakings.'[145]

CRITERIA FOR THE DETERMINATION OF EQUIVALENCE OF SUSTAINABILITY REPORTING STANDARDS

A minimum criterium to determine the equivalence is the application of the double-materiality principle in non-European standards. It means that third-country undertakings will need to report both on the impacts of their activities on people and the environment, and on how sustainability matters affect the undertaking (including but not exclusively how undertakings are financially affected).

GENERAL PRINCIPLE OF COMITOLOGY

See comment on page 106.

143 Directive (EU) 2022/2464 (CSRD).
144 CSRD, Recital 24.
145 CSRD, extract from Recital 25.

ARTICLE 28D
ESMA GUIDELINES

After consulting the European Environment Agency and the European Union Agency for Fundamental Rights, ESMA shall issue guidelines in accordance with Article 16[146] of Regulation (EU) No 1095/2010[147] on the supervision of sustainability reporting by national competent authorities.

I. ADDITIONAL TEXTS

ADDITIONAL TEXT NO. 31

Regulation (EU) No 1095/2010 of the European Parliament and the Council of 24 November 2010, ESMA Regulation, Article 16

1. The Authority shall, with a view to establishing consistent, efficient and effective supervisory practices within the European System of Financial Supervision, and to ensuring the common, uniform and consistent application of Union law, issue guidelines and recommendations addressed to competent authorities or financial market participants. Guidelines and recommendations shall be in accordance with the empowerments conferred in the legislative acts referred to in Article 1(2) or in this Article.
2. The Authority shall, where appropriate, conduct open public consultations regarding the guidelines and recommendations and analyze the related potential costs and benefits. Such consultations and analyses shall be proportionate in relation to the scope, nature and impact of the guidelines or recommendations. The Authority shall, where appropriate, also request opinions or advice from the Securities and Markets Stakeholder Group referred to in Article 37.
   [...]

2a. Guidelines and recommendations shall not merely refer to, or reproduce, elements of legislative acts. Before issuing a new guideline or recommendation,

146 'Guidelines and recommendations'.

147 See additional text No. 31, p. 119.

the Authority shall first review existing guidelines and recommendations, in order to avoid any duplication.
3. The competent authorities and financial market participants shall make every effort to comply with those guidelines and recommendations. [...]

II. COMMENTS

ROLE OF ESMA IN PROVIDING GUIDELINES FOR THE SUPERVISION OF CORPORATE SUSTAINABILITY REPORTING

'Directive 2004/109/EC assigns to national supervisors the task of enforcing compliance with corporate reporting requirements by undertakings whose securities are admitted to trading on a regulated market in the Union [...] Given the novel character of the sustainability reporting requirements, ESMA should issue guidelines for national competent authorities to promote convergent supervision of sustainability reporting by issuers subject to Directive 2004/109/EC. Those guidelines should only apply to the supervision of undertakings whose securities are admitted to trading on a regulated market in the Union.'[148]

Where appropriate, ESMA shall also request opinions or advice from the Securities and Markets Stakeholder Group. This group is an EU body composed of representatives from various stakeholders, including consumers, users of financial services, and representatives of small and medium-sized enterprises. It provides advice and opinions to ESMA on issues related to securities and financial markets, ensuring broader stakeholder engagement in regulatory decision-making processes.

[148] CSRD, extract from Recital 79.

PART III

Amendments to Directive 2006/43/EC

ARTICLE 1
SUBJECT MATTER

This Directive establishes rules concerning the statutory audit of annual and consolidated accounts and the assurance of annual and consolidated sustainability reporting.

COMMENTS

AUDIT DIRECTIVE AND CSRD DIRECTIVE

'Directive 2006/43/EC sets out rules concerning the statutory audit of annual and consolidated financial statements. It is necessary to ensure that consistent rules apply to the audit of financial statements and the assurance of sustainability reporting by the statutory auditor. Directive 2006/43/EC should apply where the assurance opinion on sustainability reporting is expressed by a statutory auditor or an audit firm.'[149]

'Member States should set out requirements that ensure the quality of the assurance of sustainability reporting carried out by independent assurance services providers and consistent outcomes in the assurance of sustainability reporting. Therefore, all independent assurance services providers should be subject to requirements that are equivalent to the requirements set out in Directive 2006/43/EC of the European Parliament and of the Council as regards the assurance of sustainability reporting, while being adapted to the characteristics of independent assurance services providers which do not carry out statutory audits. In particular, Member States should set out equivalent requirements as regards training and examination, continuing education, quality assurance systems, professional ethics, independence, objectivity, confidentiality and professional secrecy, appointment and dismissal, the organisation of the work of independent assurance services providers, investigations and sanctions, and the reporting of irregularities. This would also guarantee a level playing field among all persons and firms allowed by Member States to provide an assurance opinion on sustainability reporting, including

[149] CSRD, Recital 64.

statutory auditors. If an undertaking seeks the opinion of an accredited independent assurance services provider other than the statutory auditor on its sustainability reporting, it should not in addition need to request an assurance opinion on its sustainability reporting from the statutory auditor.'[150]

[150] CSRD, extract from Recital 61.

ARTICLE 2
DEFINITIONS

Extract

[1. 'statutory audit' means an audit of annual financial statements or consolidated financial statements in so far as:
   (a) required by Union law;
   (b) required by national law as regards small undertakings;
   (c) voluntarily carried out at the request of small undertakings which meets national legal requirements that are equivalent to those for an audit under point (b), where national legislation defines such audits as statutory audits;]
2. 'statutory auditor' means a natural person who is approved in accordance with this Directive by the competent authorities of a Member State to carry out statutory audits and, where applicable, the assurance of sustainability reporting;
3. 'audit firm' means a legal person or any other entity, regardless of its legal form, that is approved in accordance with this Directive by the competent authorities of a Member State to carry out statutory audits and, where applicable, the assurance of sustainability reporting;
4. 'third-country audit entity' means an entity, regardless of its legal form, which carries out audits of the annual or consolidated financial statements, or, where applicable, the assurance of sustainability reporting of a company incorporated in a third country, other than an entity which is registered as an audit firm in any Member State as a consequence of approval in accordance with Article 3;[151]
5. 'third-country auditor' means a natural person who carries out audits of the annual or consolidated financial statements or, where applicable, the assurance of sustainability reporting of a company incorporated in a third country, other than a person who is registered as a statutory auditor in any Member State as a consequence of approval in accordance with Articles 3 and 44;[152]

---

151 'Approval of statutory auditors and audit firms'.

152 'Approval of auditors from third countries'.

6. 'group auditor' means the statutory auditor(s) or audit firm(s) carrying out the statutory audit of the consolidated accounts or, where applicable, the assurance of consolidated sustainability reporting;

[7. 'network' means the larger structure:

- which is aimed at cooperation and to which a statutory auditor or an audit firm belongs, and
- which is clearly aimed at profit- or cost-sharing or shares common ownership, control or management, common quality-control policies and procedures, a common business strategy, the use of a common brand-name or a significant part of professional resources;

8. 'affiliate of an audit firm' means any undertaking, regardless of its legal form, which is connected to an audit firm by means of common ownership, control or management;

9. 'audit report' means the report referred to in Article 51a of Directive 78/660/EEC and Article 37 of Directive 83/349/EEC[153] issued by the statutory auditor or audit firm;

10. 'competent authorities' means the authorities designated by law that are in charge of the regulation and/or oversight of statutory auditors and audit firms or of specific aspects thereof; the reference to 'competent authority' in a specific article means a reference to the authority responsible for the functions referred to in that Article;]

[...]

16a. 'key sustainability partner(s)' means:

(a) the statutory auditor(s) designated by an audit firm for a particular assurance engagement concerning sustainability reporting as being primarily responsible for carrying out the assurance of sustainability reporting on behalf of the audit firm; or

(b) in the case of the assurance of consolidated sustainability reporting at least the statutory auditor(s) designated by an audit firm as being primarily responsible for carrying out the assurance of sustainability reporting at the level of the group and the statutory auditor(s) designated as being primarily responsible at the level of material subsidiaries; or

(c) the statutory auditor(s) who sign(s) the assurance report on sustainability reporting referred to in Article 28a;

[...]

21. 'sustainability reporting' means sustainability reporting as defined in point (18) of Article 2 of Directive 2013/34/EU;

22. 'assurance of sustainability reporting' means the performance of procedures resulting in the opinion expressed by the statutory auditor or audit firm in

---

153 Those texts have been repealed. Those two articles set the obligation of audit for companies' (consolidated) annual accounts and annual reports by a third party auditor.

accordance with point (aa) of the second subparagraph of Article 34(1) and Article 34(2) of Directive 2013/34/EU;

23. 'independent assurance services provider' means a conformity assessment body accredited in accordance with Regulation (EC) No 765/2008 of the European Parliament and of the Council[154] for the specific conformity assessment activity referred to in point (aa) of the second subparagraph of Article 34(1) of Directive 2013/34/EU.

COMMENTS

APPROVAL OF AUDITORS WITHIN THE EU

Article 3 of the Audit Directive (2006/43/EC) outlines the requirements for the approval of statutory auditors and audit firms within the EU. The directive establishes the criteria and procedures for obtaining approval, including education, professional training, and experience requirements for statutory auditors. Audit firms are required to adhere to specific quality control standards and independence requirements. National competent authorities within each EU Member State are responsible for granting approval to statutory auditors and audit firms, ensuring compliance with the directive's provisions.

APPROVAL OF AUDITORS FROM THIRD COUNTRIES

Article 44 of the Audit Directive (2006/43/EC) focuses on the approval of auditors from third countries (non-EU countries) who wish to practice within the EU. The Directive sets out the conditions and procedures for obtaining approval, which include demonstrating equivalence to EU audit regulatory standards. Third-country auditors must provide evidence of meeting criteria comparable to those required for EU auditors, including professional qualifications, experience, and adherence to international auditing standards. National competent authorities are responsible for assessing the equivalence of third-country auditor regulatory frameworks and granting approval accordingly. Cooperation and information exchange between EU Member States and third-country authorities are encouraged to facilitate the approval process and ensure regulatory alignment.

---

[154] See comment p. 12.

ARTICLE 6
EDUCATIONAL QUALIFICATIONS

1. Without prejudice to Article 11,[155] a natural person may be approved to carry out a statutory audit only after having attained university entrance or equivalent level, then completed a course of theoretical instruction, undergone practical training and passed an examination of professional competence of university final or equivalent examination level, organized or recognised by the Member State concerned.
2. A natural person may, in addition to the approval to carry out statutory audits provided for in paragraph 1 of this Article, be approved to carry out the assurance of sustainability reporting when the additional specific requirements of Article 7(2), Article 8(3), the second subparagraph of Article 10(1) and the fourth subparagraph of Article 14(2), of this Directive are met.
3. The competent authorities referred to in Article 32 shall cooperate with each other with a view to achieving a convergence of the requirements set out in this Article. When engaging in such cooperation, those competent authorities shall take into account developments in auditing and in the audit profession and, in particular, convergence that has already been achieved by the profession. They shall cooperate with the Committee of European Auditing Oversight Bodies (CEAOB) and the competent authorities referred to in Article 20[156] of Regulation (EU) No 537/2014[157] in so far as such convergence relates to the statutory audit and assurance of sustainability reporting of public-interest entities.

---

[155] 'Qualification through long-term practical experience'; following this article, a Member State may approve a person who does not satisfy the conditions laid down in Article 6 as a statutory auditor, if he or she can show either: (a) that he or she has, for 15 years, engaged in professional activities which have enabled him or her to acquire sufficient experience in the fields of finance, law and accountancy, and has passed the examination of professional competence referred to in Article 7, or (b) that he or she has, for seven years, engaged in professional activities in those fields and has, in addition, undergone the practical training referred to in Article 10 and passed the examination of professional competence referred to in Article 7.

[156] 'Designation of competent authorities'.

[157] Audit regulation.

COMMENTS

NATIONAL OVERSIGHT FOR STATUTORY AUDITORS AND AUDIT FIRMS

'Statutory auditors or audit firms that carry out the assurance of sustainability reporting should have a high level of technical and specialized expertise in the field of sustainability.'[158]

Competent authorities overseeing for statutory auditors and audit firms[159] within the Member States shall work on a convergence of theoretical, practical or other requirements needed to qualify as a statutory auditor and audit firm. They shall cooperate with the Committee of European Auditing Oversight Bodies (CEAOB).

ROLE OF THE CEAOB

Its role is to strengthen EU-wide audit oversight, which is a key objective of the new EU legislation on statutory audit that took effect on 17 June 2016. The Committee of European Auditing Oversight Bodies (CEAOB) is composed of representatives of the national audit oversight bodies of the EU and the European Securities and Markets Authority (ESMA). Representatives of the national audit authorities of the European Economic Area also participate. The European Banking Authority (EBA) and the European Insurance and Occupational Pensions Authority (EIOPA) are observers.

[158] CSRD, Recital 67.

[159] See Art. 32 of Directive 2006/43/EC and Art. 20 of Regulation (EU) No 537/2014 for listed companies.

ARTICLE 7
EXAMINATION OF PROFESSIONAL COMPETENCE

1. The examination of professional competence referred to in Article 6 shall guarantee the necessary level of theoretical knowledge of subjects relevant to statutory audit and the ability to apply such knowledge in practice. At least part of that examination shall be written.
2. In order for the statutory auditor to also be approved to carry out the assurance of sustainability reporting, the examination of professional competence referred to in Article 6 shall guarantee the necessary level of theoretical knowledge of subjects relevant to the assurance of sustainability reporting and the ability to apply such knowledge in practice. At least part of that examination shall be written.

ARTICLE 8
TEST OF THEORETICAL KNOWLEDGE

[1. The test of theoretical knowledge included in the examination shall cover the following subjects in particular:
   (a) general accounting theory and principles;
   (b) legal requirements and standards relating to the preparation of annual and consolidated accounts;
   (c) international accounting standards;
   (d) financial analysis;
   (e) cost and management accounting;
   (f) risk management and internal control;
   (g) auditing and professional skills;
   (h) legal requirements and professional standards relating to statutory audit and statutory auditors;
   (i) international auditing standards as referred to in Article 26;[160]
   (j) professional ethics and independence.
2. It shall also cover at least the following subjects insofar as they are relevant to auditing:
   (a) company law and corporate governance;
   (b) the law of insolvency and similar procedures;
   (c) tax law;
   (d) civil and commercial law;
   (e) social security law and employment law;
   (f) information technology and computer systems;
   (g) business, general and financial economics;
   (h) mathematics and statistics;
   (i) basic principles of the financial management of undertakings.]

160 'Auditing standards'.

3. In order for the statutory auditor to also be approved to carry out the assurance of sustainability reporting, the test of theoretical knowledge referred to in paragraph 1 shall also cover at least the following subjects:
   (a) legal requirements and standards relating to the preparation of annual and consolidated sustainability reporting;
   (b) sustainability analysis;
   (c) due diligence processes with regard to sustainability matters;
   (d) legal requirements and assurance standards for the sustainability reporting referred to in Article 26a.

ARTICLE 10
PRACTICAL TRAINING

[1. In order to ensure the ability to apply theoretical knowledge in practice, a test of which is included in the examination, a trainee shall complete a minimum of three years' practical training in, inter alia, the auditing of annual accounts, consolidated accounts or similar financial statements. At least two thirds of such practical training shall be completed with a statutory auditor or audit firm approved in any Member State.]

In order for the statutory auditor or the trainee to also be approved to carry out the assurance of sustainability reporting, at least eight months of the practical training referred to in the first subparagraph shall be on the assurance of annual and consolidated sustainability reporting or on other sustainability-related services.

[2. Member States shall ensure that all training is carried out with persons providing adequate guarantees regarding their ability to provide practical training.]

COMMENTS

MANDATORY PRACTICAL TRAINING FOR STATUTORY AUDITORS IN SUSTAINABILITY REPORTING

'Statutory auditors should complete practical training of at least eight months in the assurance of annual and consolidated sustainability reporting or in other sustainability-related services, taking account of previous employment experience.'[161]

[161] CSRD, extract from Recital 65.

ARTICLE 12

COMBINATION OF PRACTICAL TRAINING AND THEORETICAL INSTRUCTION

1. Member States may provide that periods of theoretical instruction in the subjects referred to in Article 8(1) and (2) shall count towards the periods of professional activity referred to in Article 11,[162] provided that such instruction is attested by an examination recognised by the Member State. Such instruction shall not last less than one year, nor may it reduce the period of professional activity by more than four years.
2. The period of professional activity and practical training shall not be shorter than the course of theoretical instruction together with the practical training required under the first subparagraph of Article 10(1).

---

[162] 'Qualification through long-term practical experience', see n. 155, p. 129.

ARTICLE 14

APPROVAL OF STATUTORY AUDITORS FROM ANOTHER MEMBER STATE

[1. The competent authorities shall establish procedures for the approval of statutory auditors who have been approved in other Member States. Those procedures shall not go beyond the requirement to complete an adaptation period as defined in point (g) of Article 3(1) of Directive 2005/36/EC of the European Parliament and of the Council or to pass an aptitude test as defined in point (h) of that provision.

2. The host Member State shall decide whether the applicant seeking approval is to be subject to an adaptation period as defined in point (g) of Article 3(1) of Directive 2005/36/EC or an aptitude test as defined in point (h) of that provision.

   The adaptation period shall not exceed three years and the applicant shall be subject to an assessment.

   The aptitude test shall be conducted in one of the languages permitted by the language rules applicable in the host Member State concerned. It shall cover only the statutory auditor's adequate knowledge of the laws and regulations of that host Member State in so far as it is relevant to statutory audits.]

   In order for the statutory auditor to also be approved to carry out the assurance of sustainability reporting, the aptitude test referred to in the first subparagraph shall cover the statutory auditor's adequate knowledge of the laws and regulations of the host Member State in so far as it is relevant to the assurance of sustainability reporting.

[3. The competent authorities shall cooperate within the framework of the CEAOB[163] with a view to achieving a convergence of the requirements of the adaptation period and the aptitude test. They shall enhance the transparency and predictability of the requirements. They shall cooperate with the CEAOB and with the competent authorities referred to in Article 20 of Regulation (EU) No 537/2014 in so far as such convergence relates to statutory audits of public-interest entities.]

---

[163] See comment p. 130.

COMMENTS

EU RECOGNITION OF PROFESSIONAL QUALIFICATIONS

Article 3(1)(g) and (h) of Directive 2005/36/EC of the European Parliament and of the Council of 7 September 2005 define key aspects of the recognition of professional qualifications in the EU. In the context of the Audit Directive, it states that procedures for the recognition of qualifications between Member States shall not go beyond the measures laid down for the recognition of professional qualifications in general.

Point (g) in particular describes the 'adaptation period', which is a supervised practice under a qualified professional in the host Member State, potentially including further training and which might be assessed. The rules and status of the migrant during this period, including rights and obligations, are determined by the host Member State's authorities.

Point (h) defines the 'aptitude test' as an assessment of the applicant's professional knowledge, skills, and competences, conducted or recognised by the host Member State's competent authority to determine their ability to practice the profession there. The test focuses on subjects not covered by the applicant's existing qualifications and may include knowledge of professional rules specific to the host Member State. Details regarding the administration of the test and the applicant's status during this preparatory period are determined by the host state's competent authority.

ARTICLE 14A
STATUTORY AUDITORS APPROVED OR RECOGNISED BEFORE 1 JANUARY 2024 AND PERSONS UNDERGOING THE APPROVAL PROCESS FOR STATUTORY AUDITORS ON 1 JANUARY 2024

Member States shall ensure that statutory auditors that are approved or recognised to carry out statutory audits before 1 January 2024 are not subject to the requirements of Article 7(2), Article 8(3), the second subparagraph of Article 10(1) and the fourth subparagraph of Article 14(2).

Member States shall ensure that persons that on 1 January 2024 are undergoing the approval process provided for in Articles 6 to 14[164] are not subject to the requirements of Article 7(2), Article 8(3), the second subparagraph of Article 10(1) and the fourth subparagraph of Article 14(2), provided they complete that process by 1 January 2026.

Member States shall ensure that statutory auditors approved before 1 January 2026 who wish to carry out the assurance of sustainability reporting acquire the necessary knowledge of sustainability reporting and the assurance of sustainability reporting, including of the subjects listed in Article 8(3), via the continuing education referred to in Article 13.[165]

---

164 See additional text No. 32, p. 142.

165 Art. 13: 'Member States shall ensure that statutory auditors are required to take part in appropriate programmes of continuing education in order to maintain their theoretical knowledge, professional skills and values at a sufficiently high level, and that failure to respect the continuing education requirements is subject to appropriate sanctions as referred to in Article 30.'

I. ADDITIONAL TEXTS

ADDITIONAL TEXT NO. 32

Directive 2006/43/EC of the European Parliament and of the Council of 17 May 2006, Audit Directive, Article 9

1. By way of derogation from Articles 7 and 8, a Member State may provide that a person who has passed a university or equivalent examination or holds a university degree or equivalent qualification in one or more of the subjects referred to in Article 8 may be exempted from the test of theoretical knowledge in the subjects covered by that examination or degree.
2. By way of derogation from Article 7, a Member State may provide that a holder of a university degree or equivalent qualification in one or more of the subjects referred to in Article 8, may be exempted from the test of the ability to apply in practice his or her theoretical knowledge of such subjects if he or she has received practical training in those subjects attested by an examination or diploma recognised by the State.

II. COMMENTS

CASE OF STATUTORY AUDITORS ALREADY APPROVED OR RECOGNISED

'The rules on the approval and recognition of statutory auditors and audit firms should allow statutory auditors to qualify also for the assurance of sustainability reporting. Member States should ensure that statutory auditors who wish to qualify for the assurance of sustainability reporting have the necessary level of theoretical knowledge of subjects relevant to the assurance of sustainability reporting and the ability to apply such knowledge in practice.

Therefore, statutory auditors should complete practical training of at least eight months in the assurance of annual and consolidated sustainability reporting or in other sustainability-related services, taking account of previous employment experience. However, statutory auditors that have already been approved or recognised in a Member State should continue to be allowed to carry out the assurance of sustainability reporting. Likewise, Member States should ensure that natural persons who are undergoing the approval process at the date of application of the requirements for the assurance of sustainability reporting established by this amending Directive are not subject to those requirements, provided they complete the process within the following two years. Member States should, however, ensure that statutory auditors approved within two years of the date of application of those requirements and who wish to carry out the assurance of sustainability reporting acquire the necessary knowledge in sustainability reporting and the assurance of sustainability reporting via continued professional education. Natural persons who decide to be approved only as statutory auditors for statutory audit should be able to decide at a later point in time to qualify also for the assurance of sustainability reporting. In order to do so, such persons should meet the necessary requirements set out by Member States to ensure that they also have the necessary level of theoretical knowledge of subjects relevant to the assurance of sustainability reporting and the ability to apply such knowledge in practice.'[166]

[166] CSRD, Recital 65.

ARTICLE 16
REGISTRATION OF STATUTORY AUDITORS

1. As regards statutory auditors, the public register shall contain at least the following information:
   (a) name, address and registration number;
   (b) if applicable, the name, address, website address and registration number of the audit firm(s) by which the statutory auditor is employed, or with whom he or she is associated as a partner or otherwise;
   (c) whether the statutory auditor is also approved for carrying out the assurance of sustainability reporting;
   (d) all other registration(s) as statutory auditor with the competent authorities of other Member States and as auditor with third countries, including the name(s) of the registration authority(ies), and, if applicable, the registration number(s), and an indication of whether the registration concerns the statutory audit, the assurance of sustainability reporting, or both.

[2. Third-country auditors registered in accordance with Article 45 shall be clearly indicated in the register as such and not as statutory auditors.]

The register shall indicate whether third-country auditors as referred to in the first subparagraph are registered for carrying out the statutory audit, the assurance of sustainability reporting, or both.

ARTICLE 17
REGISTRATION OF AUDIT FIRMS

Extract

[1. As regards audit firms, the public register shall contain at least the following information:]

[...]

(e) name and registration number of all statutory auditors employed by, or associated as partners or otherwise with, the audit firm, and an indication of whether they are also approved for carrying out the assurance of sustainability reporting;

[...]

(i) all other registration(s) as audit firm with the competent authorities of other Member States and as audit entity with third countries, including the name(s) of the registration authority(ies), and, if applicable, the registration number(s), and an indication of whether the registration concerns the statutory audit, the assurance of sustainability reporting, or both.

[...]

[2. Third-country audit entities registered in accordance with Article 45 shall be clearly indicated in the register as such and not as audit firms.]

The register shall indicate whether third-country audit entities as referred to in the first subparagraph are registered for carrying out the statutory audit, the assurance of sustainability reporting, or both.

COMMENTS

PUBLIC REGISTER AND ASSURANCE OF SUSTAINABILITY REPORTING

Directive CSRD amends Article 17 of Audit Directive and extends the requirements that need to be contained in public registers about audit firms to take into account their registration for carrying out the assurance of sustainability reporting.

ARTICLE 24B
ORGANISATION OF THE WORK

Extract

1. Member States shall ensure that, when the statutory audit is carried out by an audit firm, that audit firm designates at least one key audit partner. The audit firm shall provide the key audit partner(s) with sufficient resources and with personnel that have the necessary competence and capabilities to carry out his, her or its duties appropriately.
   Member States shall ensure that, when the assurance of sustainability reporting is carried out by an audit firm, that audit firm designates at least one key sustainability partner, who may be (one of) the key audit partner(s). The audit firm shall provide the key sustainability partner(s) with sufficient resources and with personnel that have the necessary competence and capabilities to carry out his, her or its duties appropriately.
   Securing audit and assurance quality, independence and competence shall be the main criteria when the audit firm selects the key audit partner(s) and, where applicable, the key sustainability partner(s) to be designated.
   The key audit partner(s) shall be actively involved in the carrying-out of the statutory audit. The key sustainability partner shall be actively involved in the carrying-out of the assurance of sustainability reporting.
   [...]

2a. When carrying out the assurance of sustainability reporting, the statutory auditor shall devote sufficient time to the engagement and shall assign sufficient resources to enable him or her to carry out his or her duties appropriately.
   [...]

[4. A statutory auditor or an audit firm shall maintain a client account record. Such record shall include the following data for each audit client:
   (a) the name, the address and the place of business;]
   (b) in the case of an audit firm, the name(s) of the key audit partner(s) and, where applicable, the name(s) of the key sustainability partner(s);
   (c) the fees charged for the statutory audit, the fees charged for the assurance of sustainability reporting and the fees charged for other services in any financial year.

[...]

5a. A statutory auditor or an audit firm shall create an assurance file for each assurance engagement concerning sustainability reporting.
The statutory auditor or the audit firm shall document at least the data recorded pursuant to Article 22b[167] as regards the assurance of sustainability reporting.
The statutory auditor or the audit firm shall retain any other data and documents that are of importance in support of the assurance report on sustainability reporting referred to in Article 28a and for monitoring compliance with this Directive and other applicable legal requirements as regards the assurance of sustainability reporting.
The assurance file shall be closed no later than 60 days after the date of signature of the assurance report on sustainability reporting referred to in Article 28a.
Where the same statutory auditor carries out the statutory audit of annual financial statements and the assurance of sustainability reporting, the assurance file may be included in the audit file.

6. The statutory auditor or the audit firm shall keep records of any complaints made in writing about the performance of the statutory audits carried out and about the performance of assurance engagements concerning sustainability reporting carried out.
[...]

COMMENTS

CARRYING-OUT THE SUSTAINABILITY REPORTING

'It should be ensured that the requirements imposed on auditors as regards the statutory audit and the assurance of sustainability reporting they carry out are consistent. Therefore, there should be at least one designated person who is actively involved in carrying out the assurance of sustainability reporting ('key sustainability partner'). When carrying out the assurance of sustainability reporting, statutory auditors should be required to devote sufficient time and assign sufficient resources and expertise in order to carry out their duties appropriately. The client account record should specify the fees charged for the assurance of sustainability reporting and an assurance file should be created to

[167] This article requires statutory auditors or audit firms to assess and documents whether they meet the necessary conditions of independence and objectivity, including possible threats to it. It also requires them to assess whether they have sufficient resources and capacity and that the key audit partner in charge of supervising the audit has the necessary authorisation to operate in the Member States where the company is based.

include information related to the assurance of sustainability reporting. Where the same statutory auditor carries out the statutory audit of annual financial statements and the assurance of sustainability reporting, it should be possible to include the assurance file in the audit file. However, requirements imposed on statutory auditors relating to the assurance of sustainability reporting should only apply to those statutory auditors that carry out the assurance of sustainability reporting.'[168]

[168] CSRD, Recital 66.

ARTICLE 25
AUDIT AND ASSURANCE FEES

Member States shall ensure that adequate rules are in place which provide that fees for statutory audits and the assurance of sustainability reporting:

(a) are not influenced or determined by the provision of additional services to the entity that is the subject of the statutory audit or the assurance of sustainability reporting; and

(b) cannot be based on any form of contingency.

ARTICLE 25B

PROFESSIONAL ETHICS, INDEPENDENCE, OBJECTIVITY, CONFIDENTIALITY AND PROFESSIONAL SECRECY AS REGARDS THE ASSURANCE OF SUSTAINABILITY REPORTING

The requirements in Articles 21 to 24a as regards the statutory audit of financial statements shall apply mutatis mutandis to the assurance of sustainability reporting.

COMMENTS

PROFESSIONAL ETHICS, INDEPENDENCE, OBJECTIVITY, CONFIDENTIALITY, AND PROFESSIONAL SECRECY FOR STATUTORY AUDITORS AND AUDIT FIRMS

Article 21 of Audit Directive mandates that Member States ensure statutory auditors and audit firms adhere to principles of professional ethics, emphasising the public interest, integrity, objectivity, professional competence, and due care. Auditors must maintain professional skepticism throughout audits, considering potential material misstatements from fraud or error, particularly when evaluating management estimates related to fair values, asset impairment, provisions, and future cash flow.

Article 22 requires auditors to maintain independence from audited entities during the financial statement period and audit period. Auditors must avoid conflicts of interest, ensuring no involvement in decision-making within the audited entity. They must document threats to independence and related safeguards and avoid financial interests or relationships that could compromise their impartiality. Auditors must also refrain from accepting significant gifts or favours from audited entities.

Article 22a stipulates a cooling-off period before former auditors or employees of audit firms can assume key management positions in audited entities, ensuring at least one year (two years for public-interest entities) has elapsed.

Article 22b requires auditors to assess and document compliance with independence requirements, potential threats, necessary resources, and qualifications before accepting or continuing audit engagements.

Article 23 ensures confidentiality and professional secrecy for information accessed during audits, allowing necessary information sharing with successor auditors and group auditors in third countries under specific conditions.

Article 24 protects the independence and objectivity of auditors from interference by audit firm owners, shareholders, or administrative, management, and supervisory bodies.

Article 24a outlines organisational requirements for auditors and audit firms, including policies for preventing conflicts of interest, maintaining quality control, ensuring appropriate employee knowledge, and monitoring the effectiveness of these systems. Audit firms must ensure continuity, manage incidents affecting audit integrity, and implement remuneration policies that prioritise audit quality over non-audit service revenues.

ARTICLE 25C

PROHIBITED NON-AUDIT SERVICES IN CASES WHERE THE STATUTORY AUDITOR CARRIES OUT THE ASSURANCE OF SUSTAINABILITY REPORTING OF A PUBLIC-INTEREST ENTITY

1. A statutory auditor or an audit firm carrying out the assurance of sustainability reporting of a public-interest entity, or any member of the network to which the statutory auditor or the audit firm belongs, shall not directly or indirectly provide to the public-interest entity that is the subject of the assurance of sustainability reporting, to its parent undertaking or to its controlled undertakings within the Union the prohibited non-audit services referred to in points (b) and (c) and points (e) to (k) of the second subparagraph of Article 5(1) of Regulation (EU) No 537/2014 in:
   (a) the period between the beginning of the period subject to the assurance of sustainability reporting and the issuing of the assurance report on sustainability reporting; and
   (b) the financial year immediately preceding the period referred to in point (a) of this paragraph in relation to the services referred to in point (e) of the second subparagraph of Article 5(1) of Regulation (EU) No 537/2014.
2. A statutory auditor or an audit firm carrying out the assurance of sustainability reporting of public-interest entities and, where the statutory auditor or the audit firm belongs to a network, any member of such network, may provide to the public-interest entity that is the subject of the assurance of sustainability reporting, to its parent undertaking or to its controlled undertakings non-audit services other than the prohibited non-audit services referred to in paragraph 1 of this Article, or if applicable, the prohibited non-audit services referred to in the second subparagraph of Article 5(1) of Regulation (EU) No 537/2014 or services considered by Member States to represent a threat to independence as referred to in Article 5(2) of that Regulation, subject to the approval of the audit

committee after it has properly assessed threats to independence and the safeguards applied in accordance with Article 22b[169] of this Directive.

3. When a member of a network to which the statutory auditor or the audit firm carrying out the assurance of sustainability reporting of a public-interest entity belongs provides the prohibited non-audit services referred to in paragraph 1 of this Article to an undertaking incorporated in a third country which is controlled by the public-interest entity that is the subject of assurance of sustainability reporting, the statutory auditor or the audit firm concerned shall assess whether his, her or its independence would be compromised by such provision of services by the member of the network. If his, her or its independence is affected, the statutory auditor or the audit firm shall apply safeguards in order to mitigate the threats caused by the provision of prohibited non-audit services referred to in paragraph 1 of this Article in a third country. The statutory auditor or the audit firm may continue to carry out the assurance of sustainability reporting of the public-interest entity only if he, she or it can justify, in accordance with Article 22b, that the provision of such services does not affect his, her or its professional judgment and the assurance report on sustainability reporting.

[169] 'Preparation for the statutory audit and assessment of threats to independence'; see comment p. 156.

ARTICLE 25D
IRREGULARITIES

Article 7 of Regulation (EU) No 537/2014[170] shall apply *mutatis mutandis* to a statutory auditor or an audit firm carrying out the assurance of sustainability reporting of a public-interest entity.

I. ADDITIONAL TEXTS

ADDITIONAL TEXT NO. 33

Regulation (EU) No 537/2014 of the European Parliament and of the Council of 16 April 2014, Statutory audit of public-interest entities Regulation, Article 7

Without prejudice to Article 12 of this Regulation and Directive 2005/60/EC, when a statutory auditor or an audit firm carrying out the statutory audit of a public-interest entity suspects or has reasonable grounds to suspect that irregularities, including fraud with regard to the financial statements of the audited entity, may occur or have occurred, he, she or it shall inform the audited entity and invite it to investigate the matter and take appropriate measures to deal with such irregularities and to prevent any recurrence of such irregularities in the future.

Where the audited entity does not investigate the matter, the statutory auditor or the audit firm shall inform the authorities as designated by the Member States responsible for investigating such irregularities.

The disclosure in good faith to those authorities, by the statutory auditor or the audit firm, of any irregularities referred to in the first subparagraph shall not constitute a breach of any contractual or legal restriction on disclosure of information.

170 See additional text No. 33, p. 159.

II. COMMENTS

PROHIBITION OF CERTAIN NON-AUDIT SERVICES

'To ensure the independence of the statutory auditor, certain non-audit services should also be prohibited when the statutory auditor is carrying out the assurance of sustainability reporting. Regulation (EU) No 537/2014 requires statutory auditors to report irregularities to the audited entity and, under certain circumstances, to authorities designated by the Member States as responsible for investigating such irregularities. Such obligation should also be extended, as appropriate, to statutory auditors and audit firms as regards their work on the assurance of sustainability reporting of public-interest entities.'[171]

DUTY OF VIGILANCE AND DIALOGUE WITH SUPERVISORY AUTHORITIES

Article 12 of Regulation 537/2014 requires statutory auditors or audit firms of public-interest entities to promptly report to the relevant supervisory authorities any significant breaches of laws, threats to the entity's continuity, or issues leading to an adverse or qualified audit opinion discovered during their audits. This duty also applies to audits of entities closely linked to the public-interest entity. Effective communication between auditors and supervisory authorities, particularly those supervising credit institutions and insurance undertakings, is mandated, with compliance responsibility shared by both parties. The European Systemic Risk Board (ESRB) and the Committee of European Auditing Oversight Bodies (CEAOB)[172] are to hold annual meetings with auditors of globally significant financial institutions to discuss sectoral developments. The European Banking Authority (EBA) and the European Insurance and Occupational Pensions Authority (EIOPA) shall issue guidelines to facilitate these dialogues.

171 CSRD, extract from Recital 78.

172 See comment p. 130.

ARTICLE 26A

ASSURANCE STANDARDS FOR SUSTAINABILITY REPORTING

1. Member States shall require statutory auditors and audit firms to carry out the assurance of sustainability reporting in compliance with the assurance standards adopted by the Commission in accordance with paragraph 3.
2. Member States may apply national assurance standards, procedures or requirements as long as the Commission has not adopted an assurance standard covering the same subject matter.
   Member States shall communicate the national assurance standards, procedures or requirements to the Commission at least three months before their entry into force.
3. The Commission shall, no later than 1 October 2026, adopt delegated acts in accordance with Article 48a[173] in order to supplement this Directive in order to provide for limited assurance standards setting out the procedures that the auditor(s) and the audit firm(s) shall perform in order to draw his, her or its conclusions on the assurance of sustainability reporting, including engagement planning, risk consideration and response to risks and type of conclusions to be included in the assurance report on sustainability reporting, or, where relevant, in the audit report.
   The Commission shall, no later than 1 October 2028, adopt delegated acts in accordance with Article 48a in order to supplement this Directive in order to provide for reasonable assurance standards, following an assessment to determine if reasonable assurance is feasible for auditors and for undertakings. Taking into account the results of that assessment and if therefore appropriate, those delegated acts shall specify the date from which the opinion referred to in point (aa) of the second subparagraph of Article 34(1)[174] is to be based on a reasonable assurance engagement that is based on those reasonable assurance standards.
   The Commission may adopt the assurance standards referred to in the first and second subparagraphs only if they:
   (a) have been developed with proper due process, public oversight and transparency;

[173] It precises the conditions of delegation of power to the Commission to adopt these acts.
[174] Of Directive 2013/34/EU.

(b) contribute a high level of credibility and quality to the annual or consolidated sustainability reporting; and
(c) are conducive to the Union public good.

COMMENTS

LIMITED ASSURANCE AND REASONABLE ASSURANCE

'The assurance profession distinguishes between limited assurance engagements and reasonable assurance engagements. The conclusion of a limited assurance engagement is usually provided in a negative form of expression by stating that no matter has been identified by the practitioner to conclude that the subject matter is materially misstated. In a limited assurance engagement, the auditor performs fewer tests than in a reasonable assurance engagement. The amount of work for a limited assurance engagement is therefore less than for a reasonable assurance engagement. The amount of work in a reasonable assurance engagement entails extensive procedures including consideration of internal controls of the reporting undertaking and substantive testing, and is therefore significantly greater than in a limited assurance engagement.

The conclusion of a reasonable assurance engagement is usually provided in a positive form of expression and results in providing an opinion on the measurement of the subject matter against previously defined criteria. Directive 2013/34/EU requires Member States to ensure that the statutory auditor or audit firm checks whether the non-financial statement or the separate report has been provided. It does not require that an independent provider of assurance services verify the information, although it allows Member States to require such verification where they so wish. The absence of an assurance requirement concerning sustainability reporting, in contrast to the requirement for the statutory auditor to carry out statutory audits based on a reasonable assurance engagement, would threaten the credibility of the sustainability information disclosed, thus failing to meet the needs of the intended users of that information. Although the objective is to have a similar level of assurance for financial and sustainability reporting, the absence of a commonly agreed standard for the assurance of sustainability reporting creates the risk of different understandings and expectations of what a reasonable assurance engagement would consist of for different categories of sustainability information, especially with regard to forward-looking and qualitative disclosures.

Therefore, a progressive approach to enhancing the level of the assurance required for sustainability information should be considered, starting with an obligation on the statutory auditor or audit firm to express an opinion about the compliance of the sustainability reporting with Union requirements based on a limited assurance engagement. That opinion should cover the compliance of the sustainability reporting with Union sustainability reporting standards, the process carried out by the undertaking to identify the information reported pursuant to the sustainability reporting standards and compliance with the requirement to mark up sustainability reporting. The auditor should also assess whether the undertaking's reporting complies with the reporting requirements of Article 8 of Regulation (EU) 2020/852. To ensure a common understanding and common expectations of what a reasonable assurance engagement would consist of, the statutory auditor or audit firm should be required to express an opinion based on a reasonable assurance engagement about the compliance of the sustainability reporting with Union requirements, when the Commission adopts assurance standards for reasonable assurance of sustainability reporting by means of delegated acts no later than 1 October 2028, following an assessment to determine if reasonable assurance is feasible for auditors and undertakings.

The gradual approach from limited assurance engagements to reasonable assurance engagements would also allow for the progressive development of the assurance market for sustainability information, and of undertakings' reporting practices. Finally, such gradual approach would phase in the increase in costs for reporting undertakings, given that assurance of sustainability reporting based on a reasonable assurance engagement is more costly than assurance of sustainability reporting based on a limited assurance engagement. Undertakings subject to sustainability reporting requirements should be able to decide to have an assurance opinion on their sustainability reporting based on a reasonable assurance engagement if they so wish, and in such cases they should be deemed to have complied with the obligation to have an opinion based on a limited assurance engagement. The opinion based on a reasonable assurance engagement concerning forward-looking information is only an assurance that such information has been prepared in accordance with applicable standards.'[175]

On 30 September 2024, the CEAOB has published non-binding guidelines regarding limited assurance on sustainability reporting.

---

175 CSRD, Recital 60.

ARTICLE 27A
ASSURANCE OF CONSOLIDATED SUSTAINABILITY REPORTING

1. Member States shall ensure that in the case of assurance engagements concerning the consolidated sustainability reporting of a group of undertakings:
   (a) in relation to the consolidated sustainability reporting, the group auditor bears the full responsibility for the assurance report on sustainability reporting referred to in Article 28a;
   (b) the group auditor evaluates the assurance work performed by any independent assurance services provider(s), third-country auditor(s), statutory auditor(s), third-country audit entity(ies) or audit firm(s) for the purpose of the assurance of consolidated sustainability reporting and documents the nature, timing and extent of the work performed by those auditors, including, where applicable, the group auditor's review of relevant parts of those auditors' assurance documentation; and
   (c) the group auditor reviews the assurance work performed by independent assurance services provider(s), third-country auditor(s), statutory auditor(s), third-country audit entity(ies) or audit firm(s) for the purpose of the assurance of consolidated sustainability reporting and documents it.

   The documentation retained by the group auditor shall be such as to enable the relevant competent authority to review the work of the group auditor.

   For the purposes of point (c) of the first subparagraph of this paragraph, the group auditor shall request the agreement of the independent assurance services provider(s), third-country auditor(s), statutory auditor(s), third-country audit entity(ies) or audit firm(s) concerned to the transfer of relevant documentation during the conduct of the assurance of consolidated sustainability reporting, as a condition of the reliance by the group auditor on the work of those independent assurance services provider(s), third-country auditor(s), statutory auditor(s), third-country audit entity(ies) or audit firm(s).
2. Where the group auditor is unable to comply with point (c) of the first subparagraph of paragraph 1, he, she or it shall take appropriate measures and inform the relevant competent authority.

Such measures shall, where appropriate, include carrying out additional assurance work, either directly or by outsourcing such tasks, in the relevant subsidiary.

3. Where the group auditor is subject to a quality assurance review or an investigation concerning the assurance of consolidated sustainability reporting of a group of undertakings, the group auditor shall, when requested, make available to the competent authority the relevant documentation he, she or it retains concerning the assurance work performed by the respective independent assurance services provider(s), third-country auditor(s), statutory auditor(s), third-country audit entity(ies) or audit firm(s) for the purpose of the assurance of consolidated sustainability reporting, including any working papers relevant to the assurance of consolidated sustainability reporting.

   The competent authority may request additional documentation on the assurance work performed by any statutory auditor(s) or audit firm(s) for the purpose of the assurance of consolidated sustainability reporting from the relevant competent authorities pursuant to Article 36.[176]

   Where the assurance of sustainability reporting of a parent undertaking or a subsidiary undertaking of a group of undertakings is carried out by any auditor(s) or audit entity(ies) from a third country, the competent authority may request additional documentation on the assurance work performed by any third-country auditor(s) or third-country audit entity(ies) from the relevant competent authorities from third countries through working arrangements.

   By way of derogation from the third subparagraph, where any independent assurance services provider(s), third-country auditor(s) or audit entity(ies) that have no working arrangements carried out the assurance of sustainability reporting of a parent undertaking or a subsidiary undertaking of a group of undertakings, the group auditor shall, when requested, also be responsible for ensuring proper delivery of the additional documentation on the assurance work performed by such independent assurance services provider(s), third-country auditor(s) or audit entity(ies), including the working papers relevant to the assurance of consolidated sustainability reporting. In order to ensure such delivery, the group auditor shall retain a copy of such documentation, or alternatively agree with the independent assurance services provider(s), third-country auditor(s) or audit entity(ies) that he, she or it is to be given unrestricted access to such documentation upon request, or take any other appropriate action. Where assurance working papers cannot, for legal or other reasons, be passed from a third country to the group auditor, the documentation retained by the group auditor shall include evidence that he, she or it has undertaken the appropriate procedures in order to gain access to

[176] 'Professional secrecy and regulatory cooperation between Member States'.

the assurance documentation, and in the case of impediments other than legal ones arising from the legislation of the third country concerned, evidence supporting the existence of such impediments.

COMMENTS

PROFESSIONAL SECRECY AND REGULATORY COOPERATION BETWEEN MEMBER STATES

Article 36 of Directive 2006/43/EC establishes provisions regarding professional secrecy and regulatory cooperation between Member States in the context of statutory audits.

It mandates cooperation among competent authorities of Member States responsible for approval, registration, quality assurance, inspection, and discipline, including the exchange of information and cooperation in investigations related to statutory audits and assurance. The article imposes an obligation of professional secrecy on competent authority personnel, allowing for the exchange of confidential information covered by this secrecy obligation. Competent authorities are required to supply information promptly upon request and may refuse to act on requests under specific circumstances outlined in the article, such as where sovereignty, security, or judicial proceedings are implicated. Additionally, the article allows for notification and cooperation between competent authorities when activities contrary to the directive are identified on the territory of another Member State and provides for the possibility of requesting investigations in another Member State's territory. In the context of this article and even if not explicitly mentioned here, the CEAOB (Committee of European Audit Oversight Bodies) may play a role in facilitating regulatory cooperation between competent authorities responsible for audit oversight in different Member States.

ARTICLE 28
AUDIT REPORTING

[1. The statutory auditor(s) or the audit firm(s) shall present the results of the statutory audit in an audit report. The report shall be prepared in accordance with the requirements of auditing standards adopted by the Union or Member State concerned, as referred to in Article 26.[177]

2. The audit report shall be in writing and shall:
   (a) identify the entity whose annual or consolidated financial statements are the subject of the statutory audit; specify the annual or consolidated financial statements and the date and period they cover; and identify the financial reporting framework that has been applied in their preparation;
   (b) include a description of the scope of the statutory audit which shall, as a minimum, identify the auditing standards in accordance with which the statutory audit was conducted;
   (c) include an audit opinion, which shall be either unqualified, qualified or an adverse opinion and shall state clearly the opinion of the statutory auditor(s) or the audit firm(s) as to:
      (i) whether the annual financial statements give a true and fair view in accordance with the relevant financial reporting framework; and,
      (ii) where appropriate, whether the annual financial statements comply with statutory requirements.

   If the statutory auditor(s) or the audit firm(s) are unable to express an audit opinion, the report shall contain a disclaimer of opinion;
   (d) refer to any other matters to which the statutory auditor(s) or the audit firm(s) draw(s) attention by way of emphasis without qualifying the audit opinion;]
   (e) include an opinion and a statement, both of which shall be based on the work undertaken in the course of the audit, pursuant to points (a) and (b) of the second subparagraph of Article 34(1) of Directive 2013/34/EU;
   [(f) provide a statement on any material uncertainty relating to events or conditions that may cast significant doubt about the entity's ability to continue as a going concern;

---

[177] 'Auditing standards'.

(g) identify the place of establishment of the statutory auditor(s) or the audit firm(s).

Member States may lay down additional requirements in relation to the content of the audit report.

3. Where the statutory audit was carried out by more than one statutory auditor or audit firm, the statutory auditor(s) or the audit firm(s) shall agree on the results of the statutory audit and submit a joint report and opinion. In the case of disagreement, each statutory auditor or audit firm shall submit his, her or its opinion in a separate paragraph of the audit report and shall state the reason for the disagreement.
4. The audit report shall be signed and dated by the statutory auditor. Where an audit firm carries out the statutory audit, the audit report shall bear the signature of at least the statutory auditor(s) carrying out the statutory audit on behalf of the audit firm. Where more than one statutory auditor or audit firm have been simultaneously engaged, the audit report shall be signed by all statutory auditors or at least by the statutory auditors carrying out the statutory audit on behalf of every audit firm. In exceptional circumstances Member States may provide that such signature(s) need not be disclosed to the public if such disclosure could lead to an imminent and significant threat to the personal security of any person. In any event, the name(s) of the person(s) involved shall be known to the relevant competent authorities.
5. The report of the statutory auditor or the audit firm on the consolidated financial statements shall comply with the requirements set out in paragraphs 1 to 4. In reporting on the consistency of the management report and the financial statements as required by point (e) of paragraph 2, the statutory auditor or the audit firm shall consider the consolidated financial statements and the consolidated management report. Where the annual financial statements of the parent undertaking are attached to the consolidated financial statements, the reports of the statutory auditors or the audit firms required by this Article may be combined.]

COMMENTS

AUDIT REPORT

'Directive 2006/43/EC requires statutory auditors or audit firms to present the results of their statutory audit in an audit report. Similar rules should be set out for the assurance of sustainability reporting. The results of the assurance of sustainability reporting should be presented in an assurance report. Where the same statutory auditor carries out the statutory audit of annual financial statements and the assurance of sustainability reporting, it should be possible to present the information about the assurance of sustainability reporting in the audit report.'[178]

AUDITING STANDARDS

Article 26 of the Audit Directive is situated within a broader EU regulatory framework aimed at harmonising audit practices across Member States, ensuring high-quality financial reporting, and enhancing public trust in financial statements. It aligns with the objectives of the Accounting Directive 2013/34/EC regarding financial and sustainability statement quality and public interest. This framework ensures that while there is a unified approach towards auditing standards across the EU, Member States retain some flexibility to address specific national requirements and the needs of smaller enterprises.

This article therefore outlines the framework for auditing standards that statutory auditors and audit firms in the EU must follow. It emphasises the alignment with international auditing standards to ensure uniformity, quality, and credibility in financial reporting.

In particular, key provisions are the following:

- Adoption of international standards: Member States must ensure statutory audits comply with international auditing standards adopted by the European Commission. Until the Commission adopts relevant international standards, Member States can apply their national standards.
- Definition of international auditing standards: International auditing standards include the International Standards on Auditing (ISAs), the International Standard on Quality Control (ISQC 1), and other relevant standards issued by the International Federation of Accountants (IFAC) through the International Auditing and Assurance Standards Board (IAASB).
- Commission's role in adopting standards: The Commission is authorised to adopt international auditing standards via delegated acts. Standards adopted must be developed with proper due process, public oversight, transparency, and generally accepted internationally. They must enhance the credibility and quality of financial statements in line with Directive 2013/34/EU principles, contribute to the Union public good, and not amend or supplement the requirements of Directive 2006/43/EC beyond specified articles.

---

178 CSRD, Recital 71.

MEMBER STATES' ADDITIONAL REQUIREMENTS

Member States can impose additional audit procedures or requirements beyond international standards if necessary for national legal compliance or to enhance financial statement credibility and quality. Such additional measures must be communicated to the Commission at least three months before they take effect or within three months of the adoption of a relevant international standard.

PROPORTIONALITY FOR SMALL UNDERTAKINGS

Member States can require that audits for small undertakings apply auditing standards proportionately, considering the scale and complexity of these businesses. Measures can be taken to ensure the standards are proportionately applied to small undertakings' statutory audits.

ARTICLE 28A
ASSURANCE REPORT ON SUSTAINABILITY REPORTING

1. The statutory auditor(s) or the audit firm(s) shall present the results of the assurance of sustainability reporting in an assurance report on sustainability reporting. That report shall be prepared in accordance with the requirements of assurance standards adopted by the Commission by means of the delegated acts adopted pursuant to Article 26a(3), or, pending adoption by the Commission of those assurance standards, in accordance with national assurance standards, as referred to in Article 26a(2).
2. The assurance report on sustainability reporting shall be in writing and shall:
   (a) identify the entity whose annual or consolidated sustainability reporting is the subject of the assurance engagement; specify the annual or consolidated sustainability reporting and the date and period it covers; and identify the sustainability reporting framework that has been applied in its preparation;
   (b) include a description of the scope of the assurance of sustainability reporting which shall, as a minimum, identify the assurance standards in accordance with which the assurance of sustainability reporting was conducted;
   (c) include the opinion referred to in point (aa) of the second subparagraph of Article 34(1) of Directive 2013/34/EU.
3. Where the assurance of sustainability reporting was carried out by more than one statutory auditor or audit firm, the statutory auditor(s) or the audit firm(s) shall agree on the results of the assurance of sustainability reporting and submit a joint report and opinion. In the case of disagreement, each statutory auditor or audit firm shall submit his, her or its opinion in a separate paragraph of the assurance report on sustainability reporting and shall state the reason for the disagreement.
4. The assurance report on sustainability reporting shall be signed and dated by the statutory auditor carrying out the assurance of sustainability reporting. Where an audit firm carries out the assurance of sustainability reporting, the assurance report on sustainability reporting shall bear the signature of at least the statutory auditor(s) carrying out the assurance

of sustainability reporting on behalf of the audit firm. Where more than one statutory auditor or audit firm have been simultaneously engaged, the assurance report on sustainability reporting shall be signed by all statutory auditors or at least by the statutory auditors carrying out the assurance of sustainability reporting on behalf of every audit firm. In exceptional circumstances, Member States may provide that such signature(s) need not be disclosed to the public if such disclosure could lead to an imminent and significant threat to the personal security of any person.
In any event, the name(s) of the person(s) involved shall be known to the relevant competent authorities.

5. Member States may require that, where the same statutory auditor carries out the statutory audit of annual financial statements and the assurance of sustainability reporting, the assurance report on sustainability reporting may be included as a separate section of the audit report.
6. The report of the statutory auditor or the audit firm on the consolidated sustainability reporting shall comply with the requirements set out in paragraphs 1 to 5.

ARTICLE 29
QUALITY ASSURANCE SYSTEMS

[1. Each Member State shall ensure that all statutory auditors and audit firms are subject to a system of quality assurance which meets at least the following criteria:

(a) the quality assurance system shall be organized in such a manner that it is independent of the reviewed statutory auditors and audit firms and is subject to public oversight;

(b) the funding for the quality assurance system shall be secure and free from any possible undue influence by statutory auditors or audit firms;

(c) the quality assurance system shall have adequate resources;]

(d) the persons who carry out quality assurance reviews shall have appropriate professional education and relevant experience in statutory audit and financial reporting and, where applicable, in sustainability reporting and in the assurance of sustainability reporting or in other sustainability-related services, combined with specific training on quality assurance reviews;

[(e) the selection of reviewers for specific quality assurance review assignments shall be effected in accordance with an objective procedure designed to ensure that there are no conflicts of interest between the reviewers and the statutory auditor or audit firm under review;]

(f) the scope of the quality assurance review, supported by adequate testing of selected audit files and, where applicable, assurance files, shall include an assessment of compliance with applicable auditing standards and independence requirements and, where applicable, with assurance standards, and an assessment of the quantity and quality of resources spent, of the audit fees and fees charged for the assurance of sustainability reporting, and of the internal quality control system of the audit firm;

[(g) the quality assurance review shall be the subject of a report which shall contain the main conclusions of the quality assurance review;]

(h) quality assurance reviews shall take place on the basis of an analysis of the risk and, in the case of statutory auditors and audit firms carrying out statutory audits as defined in point (a) of point 1 of Article 2 and, where applicable, carrying out assurance of sustainability reporting, at least every six years;

[(i) the overall results of the quality assurance system shall be published annually;

(j) recommendations of quality reviews shall be followed up by the statutory auditor or audit firm within a reasonable period;

(k) quality assurance reviews shall be appropriate and proportionate in view of the scale and complexity of the activity of the reviewed statutory auditor or audit firm.

If the recommendations referred to in point (j) are not followed up, the statutory auditor or audit firm shall, if applicable, be subject to the system of disciplinary actions or penalties referred to in Article 30.

2. For the purpose of point (e) of paragraph 1, at least the following criteria shall apply to the selection of reviewers:]

(a) reviewers shall have appropriate professional education and relevant experience in statutory audit and financial reporting and, where applicable, in sustainability reporting and in the assurance of sustainability reporting or in other sustainability-related services, combined with specific training on quality assurance reviews;

[(b) a person shall not be allowed to act as a reviewer in a quality assurance review of a statutory auditor or an audit firm until at least three years have elapsed since that person ceased to be a partner or an employee of, or otherwise associated with, that statutory auditor or audit firm;

(c) reviewers shall declare that there are no conflicts of interest between them and the statutory auditor and the audit firm to be reviewed.]

2a. Member States may exempt, until 31 December 2025, persons who carry out quality assurance reviews relating to the assurance of sustainability reporting from the requirement to have relevant experience in sustainability reporting and in the assurance of sustainability reporting or in other sustainability-related services.

[3. For the purpose of point (k) of paragraph 1, Member States shall require competent authorities, when undertaking quality assurance reviews of the statutory audits of annual or consolidated financial statements of medium-sized and small undertakings, to take account of the fact that the auditing standards adopted in accordance with Article 26[179] are designed to be applied in a manner that is proportionate to the scale and complexity of the business of the audited entity.]

[179] See comment p. 171.

COMMENTS

QUALITY ASSURANCE REVIEW

'Directive 2006/43/EC requires Member States to set up a system of quality assurance review of statutory auditors and audit firms. To ensure that quality assurance reviews also take place for the assurance of sustainability reporting and that the persons who carry out quality assurance reviews have appropriate professional education and relevant experience in sustainability reporting and in the assurance of sustainability reporting, that requirement to set up a system of quality assurance review should be extended to the assurance of sustainability reporting. As a transitional measure, until 31 December 2025, the persons who carry out quality assurance reviews of the assurance of sustainability reporting should be exempted from the requirement to have relevant experience in sustainability reporting and in the assurance of sustainability reporting or in other sustainability-related services.'[180]

[180] CSRD, Recital 72.

ARTICLE 30
SYSTEMS OF INVESTIGATIONS AND SANCTIONS

1. Member States shall ensure that there are effective systems of investigations and sanctions to detect, correct and prevent inadequate execution of the statutory audit and the assurance of sustainability reporting.
2. Without prejudice to their civil liability regimes, Member States shall provide for effective, proportionate and dissuasive sanctions in respect of statutory auditors and audit firms, where statutory audits or assurance of sustainability reporting are not carried out in conformity with the provisions adopted in the implementation of this Directive, and, where applicable, with Regulation (EU) No 537/2014.
   Member States may decide not to lay down rules for administrative sanctions for infringements which are already subject to national criminal law. In that event, they shall communicate to the Commission the relevant criminal law provisions.

[3. Member States shall provide that measures taken and sanctions imposed on statutory auditors and audit firms are to be appropriately disclosed to the public. Sanctions shall include the possibility of withdrawal of approval. Member States may decide that such disclosure shall not contain personal data within the meaning of point (a) of Article 2 of Directive 95/46/EC.[181]

4. By 17 June 2016 the Member States shall notify the rules referred to in paragraph 2 to the Commission. They shall notify the Commission without delay of any subsequent amendment thereto.]

[181] See additional text No. 34, p. 180; this text has been repealed by Regulation (EU) 2016/679 on the protection of general data called General Data Protection Regulation (GDPR).

ADDITIONAL TEXTS

ADDITIONAL TEXT NO. 34

Directive 95/46/EC of the European Parliament and of the Council of 24 October 1995, Data Protection Directive (no longer in force), Article 2(a)

For the purposes of this Directive:

(a) 'personal data' shall mean any information relating to an identified or identifiable natural person ('data subject'); an identifiable person is one who can be identified, directly or indirectly, in particular by reference to an identification number or to one or more factors specific to his physical, physiological, mental, economic, cultural or social identity;

ARTICLE 30A
SANCTIONING POWERS

Extract

[1. Member States shall provide for competent authorities to have the power to take and/or impose at least the following administrative measures and sanctions for breaches of the provisions of this Directive and, where applicable, of Regulation (EU) No 537/2014]

[...]

(ca) a temporary prohibition, of up to three years' duration, banning the statutory auditor, the audit firm or the key sustainability partner from carrying out the assurance of sustainability reporting and/or signing assurance reports on sustainability reporting;

[...]

(da) a declaration that the assurance report on sustainability reporting does not meet the requirements of Article 28a of this Directive;

[...]

COMMENTS

SANCTIONS REGIME WITHIN MEMBER STATES

'Directive 2006/43/EC requires Member States to have in place an investigations and sanctions regime for statutory auditors and audit firms carrying out statutory audits. That Directive also requires Member States to organise an effective system of public oversight, and to ensure that regulatory arrangements for public oversight systems permit effective cooperation at Union level in respect of Member States' oversight activities. Such requirements should be extended to statutory auditors and audit firms that conduct assurance of sustainability reporting in order to ensure the consistency of the investigations, sanctions and oversight frameworks set up for the auditor's work in the statutory audit and the assurance of sustainability reporting.'[182]

---

[182] CSRD, Recital 73.

ARTICLE 32
PRINCIPLES OF PUBLIC OVERSIGHT

[1. Member States shall organise an effective system of public oversight for statutory auditors and audit firms based on the principles set out in paragraphs 2 to 7, and shall designate a competent authority responsible for such oversight.

2. All statutory auditors and audit firms shall be subject to public oversight].

3. The competent authority shall be governed by non-practitioners who are knowledgeable in the areas relevant to statutory audit and, where applicable, to the assurance of sustainability reporting. They shall be selected in accordance with an independent and transparent nomination procedure.
[The competent authority may engage practitioners to carry out specific tasks and may also be assisted by experts when this is essential for the proper fulfilment of its tasks. In such instances, both the practitioners and the experts shall not be involved in any decision-making of the competent authority.

4. The competent authority shall have the ultimate responsibility for the oversight of:
   (a) the approval and registration of statutory auditors and audit firms;]
   (b) the adoption of standards on professional ethics, internal quality control of audit firms,
   [(c) continuing education;
   (d) quality assurance systems;
   (e) investigative and administrative disciplinary systems.

4a. Member States shall designate one or more competent authorities to carry out the tasks provided for in this Directive. Member States shall designate only one competent authority bearing the ultimate responsibility for the tasks referred in this Article except for the purpose of the statutory audit of cooperatives, savings banks or similar entities as referred to in Article 45 of Directive 86/635/EEC, or a subsidiary or legal successor of a cooperative, savings bank or similar entity as referred to in Article 45 of Directive 86/635/EEC.
Member States shall inform the Commission of their designation.
The competent authorities shall be organised in such a manner that conflicts of interests are avoided.

4b. Member States may delegate or allow the competent authority to delegate any of its tasks to other authorities or bodies designated or otherwise authorised by law to carry out such tasks.
The delegation shall specify the delegated tasks and the conditions under which they are to be carried out. The authorities or bodies shall be organised in such a manner that conflicts of interest are avoided.
Where the competent authority delegates tasks to other authorities or bodies, it shall be able to reclaim the delegated competences on a case-by-case basis.
5. The competent authority shall have the right, where necessary, to initiate and conduct investigations in relation to statutory auditors and audit firms and the right to take appropriate action.
Where a competent authority engages experts to carry out specific assignments, it shall ensure that there are no conflicts of interest between those experts and the statutory auditor or the audit firm in question. Such experts shall comply with the same requirements as those provided for in point (a) of Article 29(2).
The competent authority shall be given the powers necessary to enable it to carry out its tasks and responsibilities under this Directive.
6. The competent authority shall be transparent. This shall include the publication of annual work programmes and activity reports.
7. The system of public oversight shall be adequately funded and shall have adequate resources to initiate and conduct investigations, as referred to in paragraph 5. The funding of the public oversight system shall be secure and free from any undue influence by statutory auditors or audit firms.]

COMMENTS

SPECIFIC CASE OF COOPERATIVES AND SAVINGS BANKS

In essence, Article 45 of Council Directive 86/635/EEC of 8 December 1986 acknowledges the historical and structural differences in how public savings banks and cooperatives might be audited within different Member States, when the statutory auditing is reserved to an existing supervisory body, while still upholding stringent requirements for the auditors' qualifications and independence.

ARTICLE 36A

REGULATORY ARRANGEMENTS BETWEEN MEMBER STATES AS REGARDS THE ASSURANCE OF SUSTAINABILITY REPORTING

The requirements of Articles 34[183] and 36[184] as regards the statutory audit of financial statements shall apply mutatis mutandis to the assurance of sustainability reporting.

---

183 'Mutual recognition of regulatory arrangements between Member States'; this article establishes a legal framework for Member States (host Member States) to acknowledge and accept – with a principle of mutual recognition and the prohibition to impose additional requirements – the regulatory measures implemented by other Member States (home-country Member State) to statutory auditor or audit firm.

184 'Professional secrecy and regulatory cooperation between Member States'; see comment p. 167.

ARTICLE 37
APPOINTMENT OF STATUTORY AUDITORS OR AUDIT FIRMS

[1. The statutory auditor or audit firm shall be appointed by the general meeting of shareholders or members of the audited entity.]
The first subparagraph shall apply to the appointment of the statutory auditor or audit firm for the purpose of the assurance of sustainability reporting.

[2. Member States may allow alternative systems or modalities for the appointment of the statutory auditor or audit firm, provided that those systems or modalities are designed to ensure the independence of the statutory auditor or audit firm from the executive members of the administrative body or from the managerial body of the audited entity.]
The first subparagraph shall apply to the appointment of the statutory auditor or audit firm for the purpose of the assurance of sustainability reporting.

3. Any contractual clause restricting the choice by the general meeting of shareholders or members of the audited entity pursuant to paragraph 1 to certain categories or lists of statutory auditors or audit firms as regards the appointment of a particular statutory auditor or audit firm to carry out the statutory audit and, where applicable, the assurance of sustainability reporting of that entity shall be prohibited. Any such existing clauses shall be null and void.
Member States shall ensure that shareholders or members of large undertakings subject to Articles 19a and 29a of Directive 2013/34/EU, except undertakings referred to in point (a) of point (1) of Article 2 of that Directive,[185] and which represent more than 5% of the voting rights or 5% of the capital of the undertaking, acting individually or collectively, have the right to table a draft resolution to be adopted in the general meeting of shareholders or members, requiring that an accredited third party that does not belong to the same audit firm or network as the statutory auditor or audit firm carrying out the statutory audit prepare a report on certain elements of the sustainability reporting and that such report be made available to the general meeting of shareholders or members.

185 Public-interest entities which are listed in the EU regulated markets; see p. 9.

COMMENTS

MINORITY SHAREHOLDERS AND APPOINTMENT OF STATUTORY AUDITORS

'Pursuant to Article 6 of Directive 2007/36/EC of the European Parliament and of the Council, Member States are required to ensure that shareholders of undertakings whose securities are admitted to trading on a regulated market in the Union, acting individually or collectively, have the right to put items on the agenda of the general meeting, provided that each such item is accompanied by a justification or a draft resolution to be adopted in the general meeting, and that they have the right to table draft resolutions for items included or to be included on the agenda of a general meeting, as the case may be. Where those rights are subject to the condition that the relevant shareholder or shareholders hold a minimum stake in the undertaking, such minimum stake is not to exceed 5% of the share capital. As regards the assurance of sustainability reporting, shareholders should be able to exercise the rights set out in Article 6 of Directive 2007/36/EC in order to table draft resolutions to be adopted in the general meeting, requiring that, firstly, an accredited third party that does not belong to the same audit firm or network as the statutory auditor or audit firm carrying out the statutory audit prepare a report on certain elements of the sustainability reporting and, secondly, that such report be made available to the general meeting.

For undertakings subject to the sustainability reporting requirements introduced by this amending Directive and that do not fall within the scope of Article 6 of Directive 2007/36/EC, shareholders which represent more than 5% of the voting rights or 5% of the capital of the undertaking, acting individually or collectively, should also be given the right to table a draft resolution to be adopted in the general meeting, requiring that, firstly, an accredited third party that does not belong to the same audit firm or network as the statutory auditor or audit firm carrying out the statutory audit prepare a report on certain elements of the sustainability reporting and, secondly, that such report be made available to the general meeting.'[186]

[186] CSRD, Recital 75.

ARTICLE 38
DISMISSAL AND RESIGNATION OF STATUTORY AUDITORS OR AUDIT FIRMS

1. Member States shall ensure that statutory auditors or audit firms may be dismissed only where there are proper grounds. Divergence of opinions on accounting treatments, audit procedures or, where applicable, on sustainability reporting or assurance procedures shall not be proper grounds for dismissal.
[2. Member States shall ensure that the audited entity and the statutory auditor or audit firm inform the authority or authorities responsible for public oversight concerning the dismissal or resignation of the statutory auditor or audit firm during the term of appointment and give an adequate explanation of the reasons therefore.]
The obligation to inform provided for in the first subparagraph shall also apply to the assurance of sustainability reporting.
[3. In the case of a statutory audit of a public-interest entity, Member States shall ensure that it is permissible for:
(a) shareholders representing 5% or more of the voting rights or of the share capital;
(b) the other bodies of the audited entities when defined by national legislation; or
(c) the competent authorities referred to in Article 32 of this or designated in accordance with Article 20(1) of Regulation (EU) No 537/2014[187] or, when provided for by national law, with Article 20(2) of that Regulation,
to bring a claim before a national court for the dismissal of the statutory auditor(s) or the audit firm(s) where there are proper grounds for so doing.]
The first subparagraph shall also apply to the assurance of sustainability reporting.

---

187 Designation of competent national authorities responsible for the surveillance of the activities of the statutory auditors and audit firms carrying out statutory audit of public-interest entities.

COMMENTS

OTHER COMPETENT AUTHORITIES RESPONSIBLE FOR THE SURVEILLANCE OF STATUTORY AUDITORS AND AUDIT FIRMS CARRYING OUT STATUTORY AUDIT OF PUBLIC-INTEREST ENTITIES

Paragraph 2 of Article 20 of Regulation (EU) 537/2014 allows Member States an exception to the rule set for the designation of competent authorities responsible for enforcing the appointment of statutory auditors or audit firms by public-interest entities. Member States can delegate this responsibility to specific competent authorities established under various directives instead of the default competent authorities designated under this regulation.

The designated competent authorities that Member States can choose from include:

(a) Article 48 of Directive 2004/39/EC: Competent authorities responsible for the supervision of investment firms and securities markets under the Markets in Financial Instruments Directive (MiFID). This Directive has been repealed by the Directive called MiFID II.

(b) Article 24(1) of Directive 2004/109/EC: Competent authorities responsible for enforcing transparency requirements for issuers whose securities are admitted to trading on a regulated market under the Transparency Directive.

(c) Point (h) of Article 24(4) of Directive 2004/109/EC: Authorities involved in the further implementation of transparency obligations as specified under the Transparency Directive.

(d) Article 20 of Directive 2007/64/EC: Competent authorities overseeing payment institutions and payment services under the Payment Services Directive (PSD). This Directive has been repealed by Directive PSD II.

(e) Article 30 of Directive 2009/138/EC: Competent authorities responsible for the supervision of insurance and reinsurance undertakings under the Solvency II Directive.

(f) Article 4(1) of Directive 2013/36/EU: Competent authorities tasked with the supervision of credit institutions and investment firms under the Capital Requirements Directive (CRD IV).

This provision allows Member States to utilise existing regulatory frameworks and authorities for the oversight of statutory audits in public-interest entities, ensuring a more integrated and efficient regulatory environment.

ARTICLE 39
AUDIT COMMITTEE

Extract

[1. Member States shall ensure that each public-interest entity has an audit committee. The audit committee shall be either a stand-alone committee or a committee of the administrative body or supervisory body of the audited entity. It shall be composed of non-executive members of the administrative body and/or members of the supervisory body of the audited entity and/or members appointed by the general meeting of shareholders of the audited entity or, for entities without shareholders, by an equivalent body.

At least one member of the audit committee shall have competence in accounting and/or auditing.

The committee members as a whole shall have competence relevant to the sector in which the audited entity is operating.

A majority of the members of the audit committee shall be independent of the audited entity. The chairman of the audit committee shall be appointed by its members or by the supervisory body of the audited entity, and shall be independent of the audited entity. Member States may require the chairman of the audit committee to be elected annually by the general meeting of shareholders of the audited entity.]

[...]

4a. Member States may allow the functions assigned to the audit committee relating to sustainability reporting and relating to the assurance of sustainability reporting to be performed by the administrative or supervisory body as a whole or by a dedicated body established by the administrative or supervisory body.

[...]

[6. Without prejudice to the responsibility of the members of the administrative, management or supervisory bodies, or of other members who are appointed by the general meeting of shareholders of the audited entity, the audit committee shall, inter alia:]

(a) inform the administrative or supervisory body of the audited entity of the outcome of the statutory audit and, where applicable, of the outcome of the assurance of sustainability reporting and explain how the statutory audit and the assurance of sustainability reporting contributed to the integrity of financial reporting and sustainability reporting respectively, and what the role of the audit committee was in that process;

(b) monitor the financial and, where applicable, sustainability reporting process, including the electronic reporting process as referred to in Article 29d of Directive 2013/34/EU and the process carried out by the undertaking to identify the information reported in accordance with the sustainability reporting standards adopted pursuant to Article 29b of that Directive, and submit recommendations or proposals to ensure their integrity;

(c) monitor the effectiveness of the undertaking's internal quality control and risk management systems and, where applicable, its internal audit, regarding the financial reporting and, where applicable, sustainability reporting of the undertaking, including its electronic reporting process as referred to in Article 29d of Directive 2013/34/EU and, without breaching its independence;

(d) monitor the statutory audit of the annual and consolidated financial statements and, where applicable, the assurance of the annual and consolidated sustainability reporting, in particular its performance, taking into account any findings and conclusions by the competent authority pursuant to Article 26(6) of Regulation (EU) No 537/2014;

(e) review and monitor the independence of the statutory auditors or the audit firms in accordance with Articles 22,[188] 22a,[189] 22b,[190] 24a,[191] 24b, 25b, 25c and 25d of this Directive and with Article 6[192] of Regulation (EU) No 537/2014, and in particular the appropriateness of the provision of non-audit services to the audited entity in accordance with Article 5 of that Regulation;

[(f) be responsible for the procedure for the selection of statutory auditor(s) or audit firm(s) and recommend the statutory auditor(s) or the audit firm(s) to be appointed in accordance with Article 16[193] of Regulation (EU) No 537/2014 except when Article 16(8) of Regulation (EU) No 537/2014 is applied].

188 'Independence and objectivity'.

189 'Employment by audited entities of former statutory auditors or of employees of statutory auditors or audit firms'.

190 'Preparation for the statutory audit and assessment of threats to independence'.

191 'Internal organisation of statutory auditors and audit firms'; see comment p. 156.

192 'Preparation for the statutory audit and assessment of threats to independence'.

193 'Appointment performed by a nomination committee'.

COMMENTS

A. FIRST COMMENT

Role of the Audit Committee in Appointing Statutory Auditors

'For companies listed on stock exchanges, the directive bolsters the central role of audit committees and extends their role to the supervision of the assurance of sustainability data. Those committees usually consist of directors (non-executive members, with at least one of them being independent), will monitor the sustainability reporting process. It includes digital reporting and adherence to standards, while providing recommendations to maintain the accuracy of sustainability information and ensuring the independence of assurance providers throughout the process.'[194]

Article 16 of Regulation 537/2014 referenced here, outlines the process for appointing statutory auditors or audit firms by public-interest entities. It mandates that the audit committee recommends at least two choices for the audit engagement to the entity's administrative or supervisory body, providing a justified preference for one. This recommendation must be free from third-party influence and comply with a selection procedure, which involves inviting proposals from audit firms, preparing tender documents, and evaluating proposals based on transparent criteria. Exceptions to this process apply under certain conditions, such as for entities meeting specific criteria or using alternative systems. Additionally, any contractual clauses limiting auditor choice are void, and public-interest entities must report any improper influence attempts to competent authorities. Member States may also impose additional requirements, like mandating multiple auditors, and can delegate audit committee functions to nomination committees under certain conditions. Subparagraph 8 in particular allows Member States to permit a nomination committee, significantly influenced by shareholders or members and responsible for auditor selection recommendations, to perform the functions of the audit committee as outlined in the article. This nomination committee must then submit the recommendation for the appointment of auditors to the general meeting of shareholders or members.

[194] CSRD Essentials.

B. SECOND COMMENT

Transparency Report by Audit Firms and Inspection

The Transparency report is mandated to provide comprehensive information regarding the firm's ownership structure, governance, quality control policies, and any other relevant details affecting the independence and integrity of its audit activities. Essentially, the transparency report serves to enhance accountability and public trust by offering stakeholders insight into the operations and safeguards implemented by audit firms to uphold professional standards and ethical conduct in their auditing practices.

While the audit committee does not conduct inspections, it plays a crucial role in the audit process for public-interest entities. It can for instance ensure the appointment of auditors is based on a fair and transparent selection process. Inspections rather are undertaken by relevant public authorities which assess the contents of the most recent annual transparency report published by auditors or audit firms.

Article 26 of Regulation (EU) No 537/2014 outlines quality assurance measures for audit firms. Subparagraph 6 in particular specifies the scope of inspections conducted by competent authorities, which must encompass evaluating the internal quality control system's design, conducting compliance testing of procedures, and reviewing audit files of public-interest entities to ensure the efficacy of the internal quality control system.

ARTICLE 45
REGISTRATION AND OVERSIGHT OF THIRD-COUNTRY AUDITORS AND AUDIT ENTITIES

Extract

1. The competent authorities of a Member State shall, in accordance with Articles 15,[195] 16 and 17 of this Directive, register every third-country auditor and audit entity, where that third-country auditor or audit entity provides an audit report concerning the annual or consolidated financial statements, or, where applicable, an assurance report concerning the annual or consolidated sustainability reporting of an undertaking incorporated outside the Union whose transferable securities are admitted to trading on a regulated market of that Member State, defined in point (21) of Article 4(1) of Directive 2014/65/EU of the European Parliament and of the Council,[196] except where the undertaking in question is an issuer exclusively of outstanding debt securities for which one of the following applies:
   (a) such securities have been admitted to trading on a regulated market in a Member State, defined in point (21) of Article 4(1) of Directive 2014/65/EU prior to 31 December 2010 and the denomination per unit of which is, at the date of issue, at least EUR 50 000 or, in the case of debt securities denominated in another currency, equivalent, at the date of issue, to at least EUR 50 000;
   (b) such securities are admitted to trading on a regulated market in a Member State, defined in point (21) of Article 4(1) of Directive 2014/65/EU from 31 December 2010 and the denomination per unit of which is, at the date of issue, at least EUR 100 000 or, in case of debt securities denominated in another currency, equivalent, at the date of issue, to at least EUR 100 000.

[...]

---

195 'Public register'.

196 See additional text No. 35, p. 198.

4. Without prejudice to Article 46,[197] audit reports concerning annual accounts or consolidated accounts or, where applicable, the assurance reports concerning annual or consolidated sustainability reporting referred to in paragraph 1 of this Article issued by third-country auditors or audit entities that are not registered in the Member State shall have no legal effect in that Member State.
5. A Member State may register a third-country audit entity for the purpose of the audit of financial statements only if:
   (a) the majority of the members of the administrative or management body of the third-country audit entity meet requirements which are equivalent to those laid down in Articles 4[198] to 10, with the exception of Article 7(2), Article 8(3) and the second subparagraph of Article 10(1);
   (b) the third-country auditor carrying out the audit on behalf of the third-country audit entity meets requirements which are equivalent to those laid down in Articles 4 to 10, with the exception of Article 7(2), Article 8(3) and the second subparagraph of Article 10(1);
   (c) the audits of the annual or consolidated financial statements referred to in paragraph 1 of this Article are carried out in accordance with international auditing standards as referred to in Article 26,[199] as well as the requirements laid down in Articles 22,[200] 22b[201] and 25, or with equivalent standards and requirements;
   (d) the third-country audit entity publishes on its website an annual transparency report which includes the information referred to in Article 13 of Regulation (EU) No 537/2014 or it complies with equivalent disclosure requirements.

   A Member State may register a third-country audit entity for the purpose of the assurance of sustainability reporting only if:
   (a) the majority of the members of the administrative or management body of the third-country audit entity meet requirements which are equivalent to those laid down in Articles 4 to 10;
   (b) the third-country auditor carrying out the assurance on behalf of the third-country audit entity meets requirements which are equivalent to those laid down in Articles 4 to 10;
   (c) the assurance of the annual or consolidated sustainability reporting referred to in paragraph 1 is carried out in accordance with the assurance standards referred to in Article 26a, as well as the requirements laid

197 'Derogation in the case of equivalence'.
198 'Good repute'.
199 See comment p. 194.
200 'Independence and objectivity'.
201 'Preparation for the statutory audit and assessment of threats to independence'; see comment p. 156.

down in Articles 22, 22b, 25 and 25b, or with equivalent standards and requirements;

(d) the third-country audit entity publishes on its website an annual transparency report which includes the information referred to in Article 13[202] of Regulation (EU) No 537/2014 or it complies with equivalent disclosure requirements.

5a. A Member State may register a third-country auditor for the purpose of the audit of financial statements only if he or she meets the requirements set out in points (b), (c) and (d) of the first subparagraph of paragraph 5 of this Article.

A Member State may register a third-country auditor for the purpose of the assurance for sustainability reporting only if he or she meets the requirements set out in points (b), (c) and (d) of the second subparagraph of paragraph 5 of this Article.

6. In order to ensure uniform conditions for the application of point (c) of the first subparagraph of paragraph 5 and point (c) of the second subparagraph of paragraph 5 of this Article, the Commission shall be empowered to decide upon the equivalence referred to therein by means of implementing acts. Those implementing acts shall be adopted in accordance with the examination procedure referred to in Article 48(2).[203]

Member States may assess the equivalence referred to point (c) of the first subparagraph of paragraph 5 and point (c) of the second subparagraph of paragraph 5 of this Article, as long as the Commission has not taken any such decision.

The Commission shall be empowered to adopt delegated acts in accordance with Article 48a supplementing this Directive for the purpose of establishing the general equivalence criteria to be used in assessing whether the audits of the financial statements and, where applicable, the assurance of sustainability reporting referred to in paragraph 1 of this Article are carried out in accordance with international auditing standards as defined in Article 26 and with assurance standards for sustainability reporting referred to in Article 26a, respectively, and with the requirements laid down in Articles 22, 24[204] and 25. Such criteria, which are applicable to all third countries, shall be used by Member States when assessing equivalence at national level.

202 'Transparency report'.

203 'Committee procedure'; see comment p. 106.

204 See comment p. 156.

I. ADDITIONAL TEXTS

ADDITIONAL TEXT NO. 35

Directive 2014/65/EU of the European Parliament and of the Council of 15 May 2014, Markets in Financial Instruments (MiFID II), point (21) of Article 4(1)

'Regulated market' means a multilateral system operated and/or managed by a market operator, which brings together or facilitates the bringing together of multiple third-party buying and selling interests in financial instruments – in the system and in accordance with its non-discretionary rules – in a way that results in a contract, in respect of the financial instruments admitted to trading under its rules and/or systems, and which is authorised and functions regularly and in accordance with Title III of this Directive;

II. COMMENTS

A. FIRST COMMENT

Registration of a Third-Country Audit Entity for the Purpose of the Assurance of Sustainability Reporting

In the context of Article 45 of Directive 2006/43/EC, these requirements ensure that third-country audit entities, when registered for sustainability reporting assurance, meet equivalent standards. Specifically, Article 45 allows Member States to register third-country audit entities only if the majority of the members of their administrative or management bodies meet requirements equivalent to those outlined in Articles 4 to 10. This ensures that third-country auditors possess the same level of professional competence, reputation, and practical experience as their EU counterparts, thereby maintaining the integrity and reliability of sustainability reporting within the EU.

In particular:

- Article 4 mandates that competent authorities may grant approval only to natural persons or firms of good repute;
- Article 5 outlines the circumstances under which approval of a statutory auditor or audit firm must be withdrawn, including serious compromise of good repute or failure to meet specified conditions. Member States are allowed to provide a reasonable period for rectification in such cases, and withdrawal must be communicated to relevant authorities in other Member States;

- Article 6 on educational qualifications stipulates the prerequisites for approval, requiring completion of university-level education, theoretical instruction, practical training, and passing a professional competence examination;
- Article 7 ensures that the examination of professional competence guarantees the necessary theoretical knowledge and practical application skills for statutory audit, with at least part of the examination being written;
- Article 8 details the subjects covered in the theoretical knowledge test of the examination, including accounting theory, legal requirements, auditing standards, financial analysis, and professional ethics. The Commission holds the authority to adjust this list as needed, considering developments in auditing and the profession; and
- Articles 9 and 10 provide exemptions and requirements regarding practical training, respectively.

Some conditions which are specific to the professional competence of assurance of sustainability reporting do not apply to the registration and oversight of third-country auditors and audit entities.

Derogation

Furthermore, regarding Article 46 of Directive 2006/43/EC, Member States can address derogations in cases where equivalence between the EU and non-EU jurisdictions is recognised.[205] In simpler terms, this means that if a non-EU country's auditing standards are considered equivalent to those in the EU, then audit reports on annual or consolidated accounts, as well as assurance reports on sustainability reporting, from that country may be accepted in the EU without requiring additional auditing. This provision helps to facilitate cross-border business transactions by streamlining auditing requirements between the EU and countries with equivalent standards.

B. SECOND COMMENT

Records

Article 15 of Regulation 537/2014 mandates that statutory auditors and audit firms retain certain documents and information for at least five years. This includes records referred to in various articles of the Regulation and Directive 2006/43/EC, covering aspects like audit procedures, quality control, and transparency. Member States have the discretion to extend this retention period, provided it aligns with their rules on personal data protection and administrative and judicial proceedings.

---

205 See comment p. 127.

ARTICLE 48A
EXERCISE OF THE DELEGATION

Extract

[...]

2. The power to adopt delegated acts referred to in Article 26a(2) shall be conferred on the Commission for an indeterminate period of time.
3. The delegation of power referred to in Article 26(3),[206] Article 26a(3), Article 45(6), Article 46(2)[207] and Article 47(3)[208] may be revoked at any time by the European Parliament or by the Council. A decision to revoke shall put an end to the delegation of the power specified in that decision. It shall take effect the day following the publication of the decision in the Official Journal of the European Union or at a later date specified therein. It shall not affect the validity of any delegated acts already in force.
   [...]
5. A delegated act adopted pursuant to Article 26(3), Article 26a(3), Article 45(6), Article 46(2) or Article 47(3) shall enter into force only if no objection has been expressed either by the European Parliament or the Council within a period of four months of notification of that act to the European Parliament and the Council or if, before the expiry of that period, the European Parliament and the Council have both informed the Commission that they will not object. That period shall be extended by two months at the initiative of the European Parliament or of the Council.

COMMENTS

See comment on page 106.

206 'Auditing standards'; see comment p. 171.

207 'Derogation in the case of equivalence', see comment p. 199.

208 'Cooperation with competent authorities from third countries'.

PART IV

Amendments to Regulation (EU) 537/2014

ARTICLE 4
AUDIT FEES

Extract

[...]

[2. When the statutory auditor or the audit firm provides to the audited entity, its parent undertaking or its controlled undertakings, for a period of three or more consecutive financial years, non-audit services other than those referred to in Article 5(1) of this Regulation, the total fees for such services shall be limited to no more than 70% of the average of the fees paid in the last three consecutive financial years for the statutory audit(s) of the audited entity and, where applicable, of its parent undertaking, of its controlled undertakings and of the consolidated financial statements of that group of undertakings.] For the purposes of the limits specified in the first subparagraph of this paragraph, the assurance of sustainability reporting, and non-audit services other than those referred to in Article 5(1), required by Union or national legislation, shall be excluded.

[...]

COMMENTS

CALCULATION OF FEES

Regulation (EU) No 537/2014 applies to statutory auditors and audit firms carrying out statutory audits of public-interest entities. To ensure the independence of the statutory auditor when carrying out a statutory audit, this Regulation sets a limit concerning the fees for other services that the statutory auditor can obtain. It is important to clarify that the assurance of sustainability reporting should not count in the calculation of this limit.

ARTICLE 5
PROHIBITION OF THE PROVISION OF NON-AUDIT SERVICES

Extract

[1. A statutory auditor or an audit firm carrying out the statutory audit of a public-interest entity, or any member of the network to which the statutory auditor or the audit firm belongs, shall not directly or indirectly provide to the audited entity, to its parent undertaking or to its controlled undertakings within the Union any prohibited non-audit services in:

(a) the period between the beginning of the period audited and the issuing of the audit report; and

(b) the financial year immediately preceding the period referred to in point (a) in relation to the services listed in point (e) of the second subparagraph.

For the purposes of this Article, prohibited non-audit services shall mean:

(a) tax services relating to:

(i) preparation of tax forms;

(ii) payroll tax;

(iii) customs duties;

(iv) identification of public subsidies and tax incentives unless support from the statutory auditor or the audit firm in respect of such services is required by law;

(v) support regarding tax inspections by tax authorities unless support from the statutory auditor or the audit firm in respect of such inspections is required by law;

(vi) calculation of direct and indirect tax and deferred tax;

(vii) provision of tax advice;

(b) services that involve playing any part in the management or decision-making of the audited entity;]

(c) bookkeeping and preparing accounting records and financial statements as well as preparing sustainability reporting;

[(d) payroll services;

(e) designing and implementing internal control or risk management procedures related to the preparation and/or control of financial information or designing and implementing financial information technology systems;
(f) valuation services, including valuations performed in connection with actuarial services or litigation support services;
(g) legal services, with respect to:
  (i) the provision of general counsel;
  (ii) negotiating on behalf of the audited entity; and
  (iii) acting in an advocacy role in the resolution of litigation;
(h) services related to the audited entity's internal audit function;
(i) services linked to the financing, capital structure and allocation, and investment strategy of the audited entity, except providing assurance services in relation to the financial statements, such as the issuing of comfort letters in connection with prospectuses issued by the audited entity;
(j) promoting, dealing in, or underwriting shares in the audited entity;
(k) human resources services, with respect to:
  (i) management in a position to exert significant influence over the preparation of the accounting records or financial statements which are the subject of the statutory audit, where such services involve:
    - searching for or seeking out candidates for such position; or
    - undertaking reference checks of candidates for such positions;
  (ii) structuring the organization design; and
  (iii) cost control.

2. Member States may prohibit services other than those listed in paragraph 1 where they consider that those services represent a threat to independence. Member States shall communicate to the Commission any additions to the list in paragraph 1.]

[...]

[4. A statutory auditor or an audit firm carrying out statutory audits of public-interest entities and, where the statutory auditor or the audit firm belongs to a network, any member of such network, may provide to the audited entity, to its parent undertaking or to its controlled undertakings non-audit services other than the prohibited non-audit services referred to in paragraphs 1 and 2 subject to the approval of the audit committee after it has properly assessed threats to independence and the safeguards applied in accordance with Article 22b[209] of Directive 2006/43/EC.]

---

209 'Preparation for the statutory audit and assessment of threats to independence'; see comment p. 156.

The approval of the audit committee referred to in the first subparagraph shall not be needed for the provision of assurance of sustainability reporting. [Member States may establish stricter rules setting out the conditions under which a statutory auditor, an audit firm or a member of a network to which the statutory auditor or audit firm belongs may provide to the audited entity, to its parent undertaking or to its controlled undertakings non-audit services other than the prohibited non-audit services referred to in paragraph 1.]

COMMENTS

SPECIFIC NON-AUDIT SERVICES ARE PROHIBITED

Regulation (EU) No 537/2014 prohibits auditors from providing certain non-audit services during specified periods when conducting statutory audits. Services related to the preparation of sustainability reports, including consulting services, are also prohibited during these periods. This prohibition applies whenever an auditor is performing a statutory audit of financial statements.

To maintain the auditor's independence, specific non-audit services should also be prohibited when they are providing assurance on sustainability reporting. Regulation (EU) No 537/2014 mandates that auditors report any irregularities to the audited entity and, under certain conditions, to designated authorities responsible for investigating these irregularities. This reporting obligation is extended to auditors and audit firms regarding the assurance of public-interest entities sustainability reporting.

PART V

Transposition and implementation of Directive (EU) 2022/2464

ARTICLE 5
TRANSPOSITION

1. Member States shall bring into force the laws, regulations and administrative provisions necessary to comply with Articles 1 to 3 of this Directive[210] by 6 July 2024. They shall immediately communicate the text of those measures to the Commission.
2. Member States shall apply the measures necessary to comply with Article 1,[211] with the exception of point (14):[212]
   (a) for financial years starting on or after 1 January 2024:
      (i) to large undertakings within the meaning of Article 3(4) of Directive 2013/34/EU[213] which are public-interest entities as defined in point (1) of Article 2 of that Directive exceeding on their balance sheet dates the average number of 500 employees during the financial year;
      (ii) to public-interest entities as defined in point (1) of Article 2 of Directive 2013/34/EU which are parent undertakings of a large group within the meaning of Article 3(7) of that Directive[214] exceeding on its balance sheet dates, on a consolidated basis, the average number of 500 employees during the financial year;
   (b) for financial years starting on or after 1 January 2025:
      (i) to large undertakings within the meaning of Article 3(4) of Directive 2013/34/EU, other than those referred to in point (a)(i) of this subparagraph;

210 (EU) 2022/2464.

211 Of Directive (EU) 2022/2464 which is presented in Part I of this book called 'Amendments to Directive 2013/34/EU'.

212 Reporting concerning third-country undertakings; see pp. 89–100.

213 Art. 3(4): 'Large undertakings shall be undertakings which on their balance sheet dates exceed at least two of the three following criteria:
(a) balance sheet total: EUR 25 000 000;
(b) net turnover: EUR 50 000 000;
(c) an average number of employees during the financial year: 250.'

214 Art. 3(7): 'Large groups shall be groups consisting of parent and subsidiary undertakings to be included in a consolidation and which, on a consolidated basis, exceed the limits of at least two of the three following criteria on the balance sheet date of the parent undertaking:
(a) balance sheet total: EUR 25 000 000;
(b) net turnover: EUR 50 000 000;
(c) an average number of employees during the financial year: 250.'

(ii) to parent undertakings of a large group within the meaning of Article 3(7) of Directive 2013/34/EU, other than those referred to in point (a)(ii) of this subparagraph;

(c) for financial years starting on or after 1 January 2026:

(i) to small and medium-sized undertakings within the meaning of Article 3(2) and (3) of Directive 2013/34/EU;[215] which are public-interest entities as defined in point (a) of point (1) of Article 2 of that Directive and which are not micro-undertakings as defined in Article 3(1) of that Directive;[216]

(ii) to small and non-complex institutions defined in point (145) of Article 4(1) of Regulation (EU) No 575/2013[217] provided they are large undertakings within the meaning of Article 3(4) of Directive 2013/34/EU or that they are small and medium sized undertakings within the meaning of Article 3(2) and (3) of that Directive which are public-interest entities as defined in point (a) of point (1) of Article 2 of that Directive and which are not micro-undertakings as defined in Article 3(1) of that Directive;

(iii) to captive insurance undertakings defined in point (2) of Article 13 of Directive 2009/138/EC[218] of the European Parliament and of the Council, and captive reinsurance undertakings defined in point (5) of Article 13 of that Directive,[219] provided that they are large undertakings within the meaning of Article 3(4) of Directive 2013/34/EU or

---

215 Art. 3(2) and (3): 'Small undertakings shall be undertakings which on their balance sheet dates do not exceed the limits of at least two of the three following criteria:
(a) balance sheet total: EUR 5 000 000;
(b) net turnover: EUR 10 000 000;
(c) average number of employees during the financial year: 50.
Member States may define thresholds exceeding the thresholds in points (a) and (b) of the first subparagraph. However, the thresholds shall not exceed EUR 7 500 000 for the balance sheet total and EUR 15 000 000 for the net turnover.
Medium-sized undertakings shall be undertakings which are not micro-undertakings or small undertakings and which on their balance sheet dates do not exceed the limits of at least two of the three following criteria:
(a) balance sheet total: EUR 25 000 000;
(b) net turnover: EUR 50 000 000;
(c) average number of employees during the financial year: 250.'

216 Art. 3(1): '[...] undertakings which on their balance sheet dates do not exceed the limits of at least two of the three following criteria:
(a) balance sheet total: EUR 450 000;
(b) net turnover: EUR 900 000;
(c) average number of employees during the financial year: 10.'

217 See additionnal text No. 8, p. 25.

218 It is a wholly-owned subsidiary created to provide insurance to its non-insurance parent company (or companies). Captives are a form of self-insurance; see additional text No. 9, p. 26.

219 See additionnal text No. 9, p. 26.

that they are small and medium sized undertakings within the meaning of Article 3(2) and (3) of that Directive which are public-interest entities as defined in point (a) of point (1) of Article 2 of that Directive and which are not micro-undertakings as defined in Article 3(1) of that Directive.

Member States shall apply the measures necessary to comply with point (14) of Article 1[220] for financial years starting on or after 1January 2028.

Member States shall apply the measures necessary to comply with Article 2:[221]

(a) for financial years starting on or after 1 January 2024:
   (i) to issuers as defined in point (d) of Article 2(1) of Directive 2004/109/EC[222] which are large undertakings within the meaning of Article 3(4) of Directive 2013/34/EU exceeding on their balance sheet dates the average number of 500 employees during the financial year;
   (ii) to issuers as defined in point (d) of Article 2(1) of Directive 2004/109/EC which are parent undertakings of a large group within the meaning of Article 3(7) of Directive 2013/34/EU exceeding on its balance sheet dates, on a consolidated basis, the average number of 500 employees during the financial year;
(b) for financial years starting on or after 1 January 2025:
   (i) to issuers as defined in point (d) of Article 2(1) of Directive 2004/109/EC which are large undertakings within the meaning of Article 3(4) of Directive 2013/34/EU other than those referred to in point (a)(i) of this subparagraph;
   (ii) to issuers as defined in point (d) of Article 2(1) of Directive 2004/109/EC which are parent undertakings of a large group within the meaning of Article 3(7) of Directive 2013/34/EU other than those referred to in point (a)(ii) of this subparagraph;
(c) for financial years starting on or after 1 January 2026:
   (i) to issuers as defined in point (d) of Article 2(1) of Directive 2004/109/EC which are small and medium-sized undertakings within the meaning of Article 3(2) and (3) of Directive 2013/34/EU and which are not micro-undertakings as defined in Article 3(1) of Directive 2013/34/EU;
   (ii) to issuers defined as small and non-complex institutions in point (145) of Article 4(1) of Regulation (EU) No 575/2013, provided they are large undertakings within the meaning of Article 3(4) of Direc-

220 Reporting concerning third-country undertakings; see pp. 89–100.

221 Of Directive (EU) 2022/2464 which is presented in Part II of this book called 'Amendments to Directive 2004/109/EC'.

222 Issuer means a legal entity governed by private or public law, including a State, whose securities are admitted to trading on a regulated market, the issuer being, in the case of depository receipts representing securities, the issuer of the securities represented.

tive 2013/34/EU or that they are small and medium-sized undertakings within the meaning of Article 3(2) and (3) of that Directive which are public-interest entities as defined in point (a) of point (1) of Article 2 of that Directive and which are not micro-undertakings as defined in Article 3(1) of that Directive;

(iii) to issuers defined as captive insurance undertakings in point (2) of Article 13 of Directive 2009/138/EC, or as captive reinsurance undertakings in point (5), of Article 13 of that Directive, provided that they are large undertakings within the meaning of Article 3(4) of Directive 2013/34/EU or that they are small and medium-sized undertakings within the meaning of Article 3(2) and (3) of that Directive which are public-interest entities as defined in point (a) of point (1) of Article 2 of that Directive and which are not micro-undertakings as defined in Article 3(1) of that Directive.

Member States shall apply the measures necessary to comply with Article 3[223] for financial years starting on or after 1 January 2024.

3. When Member States adopt the measures referred to in paragraph 1, they shall contain a reference to this Directive or shall be accompanied by such a reference on the occasion of their official publication. Member States shall determine how such reference is to be made.
4. Member States shall communicate to the Commission the text of the main provisions of national law which they adopt in the field covered by this Directive.

COMMENTS

WHAT ARE SMALL AND NON-COMPLEX INSTITUTIONS?

They are a specific category of credit institutions and investment firms, which can be subject to less stringent regulatory requirements provided they meet certain criteria.

These generally include:

- simpler operations;
- a limited size;
- a lower risk profile;
- a total asset value equal to or less than EUR 5 billion on average over the four-year period immediately preceding the current fiscal year;
- no complex or international operations;
- a straightforward organisational structure and business model; and
- limited trading activity.

223 Of Directive (EU) 2022/2464 which is presented in Part III of this book called 'Amendments to Directive 2006/43/EC'.

CSRD, WHO AND WHEN?

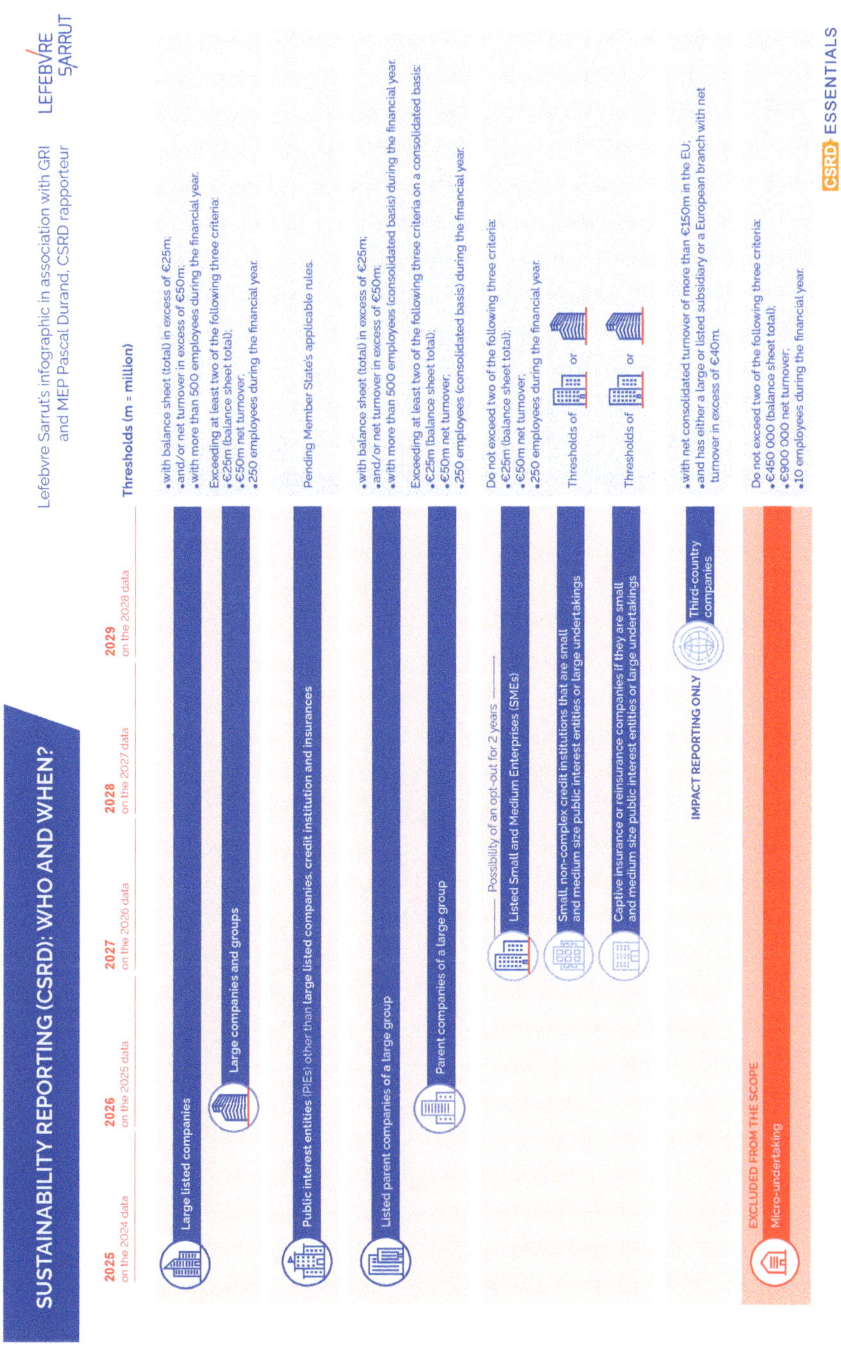

ARTICLE 6
REVIEW AND REPORTING

1. The Commission shall submit a report to the European Parliament and to the Council on the implementation of this amending Directive, including, inter alia:
   (a) an assessment of the achievement of the goals of this amending Directive, including the convergence of reporting practices between Member States;
   (b) an assessment of the number of small and medium-sized undertakings voluntarily using the sustainability reporting standards referred to in Article 29c of Directive 2013/34/EU;
   (c) an assessment of whether and how the scope of the provisions amended by this amending Directive should be further extended, in particular in relation to small and medium-sized undertakings and to third-country undertakings operating directly on the Union internal market without a subsidiary or a branch on the territory of the Union;
   (d) an assessment of the implementation of the reporting requirements on subsidiaries and branches of third-country undertakings introduced by this amending Directive, including an assessment of the number of third-country undertakings which have a subsidiary undertaking or a branch reporting in accordance with Article 40a of Directive 2013/34/EU; an assessment of the enforcement mechanism and of the thresholds set out in that Article;
   (e) an assessment of whether and how to ensure the accessibility for persons with disabilities to the sustainability reports published by undertakings falling under the scope of this amending Directive.

   The report shall be published by 30 April 2029 and every three years thereafter, and shall be accompanied, if appropriate, by legislative proposals.
2. By 31 December 2028, the Commission shall review and report on the level of concentration of the sustainability assurance market. That review shall take into account the national regimes applicable to independent assurance services providers and assess whether and to what extent those national regimes contribute to opening up the assurance market.

   By 31 December 2028, the Commission shall assess possible legal measures to ensure sufficient diversification of the sustainability assurance market and appropriate sustainability reporting quality. The Commission shall review the

measures provided for in Article 34 of Directive 2013/34/EU and assess the need to extend them to other large undertakings.
The report shall be transmitted to the European Parliament and the Council by 31 December 2028 and shall be accompanied, if appropriate, by legislative proposals.

COMMENTS

REQUIREMENTS FOR THE REPORT ON THE IMPLEMENTATION OF CSRD

'The Commission should submit a report to the European Parliament and to the Council on the implementation of this amending Directive, including, inter alia: an assessment of the achievement of the goals of this amending Directive, including the convergence of reporting practices between Member States; an assessment of the number of small and medium-sized undertakings using sustainability reporting standards voluntarily; an assessment of whether and how the scope of the reporting requirements should be further extended, in particular in relation to small and medium-sized undertakings and to third-country undertakings operating directly on the Union internal market without a subsidiary undertaking or a branch on the territory of the Union; an assessment of the implementation of the reporting requirements on subsidiary undertakings and branches of third-country undertakings introduced by this amending Directive, including an assessment of the number of third-country undertakings which have a subsidiary undertaking or a branch subject to reporting requirements in accordance with Directive 2013/34/EU; an assessment of the enforcement mechanism and of the relevant thresholds set out in Directive 2013/34/EU; an assessment of whether and how to ensure the accessibility for people with disabilities to the sustainability reporting published by undertakings falling under the scope of this amending Directive.

The report on the implementation of this amending Directive should be published by 30 April 2029 and every three years thereafter, and should be accompanied, if appropriate, by legislative proposals. By 31 December 2028, the Commission should review and report on the level of concentration of the sustainability assurance market. The review should take into account the national regimes applicable to independent assurance services providers and assess whether and to what extent such national regimes contribute to opening up the assurance market. By 31 December 2028, the Commission should assess possible legal measures to ensure sufficient diversification of the sustainability assurance market and appropriate sustainability reporting quality. The report on the level of concentration of the sustainability assurance market should be transmitted to the European Parliament and the Council by 31 December 2028 and be accompanied, if appropriate, by legislative proposals.'[224]

[224] CSRD, Recital 81.

CSRD, WHICH TIMELINE?

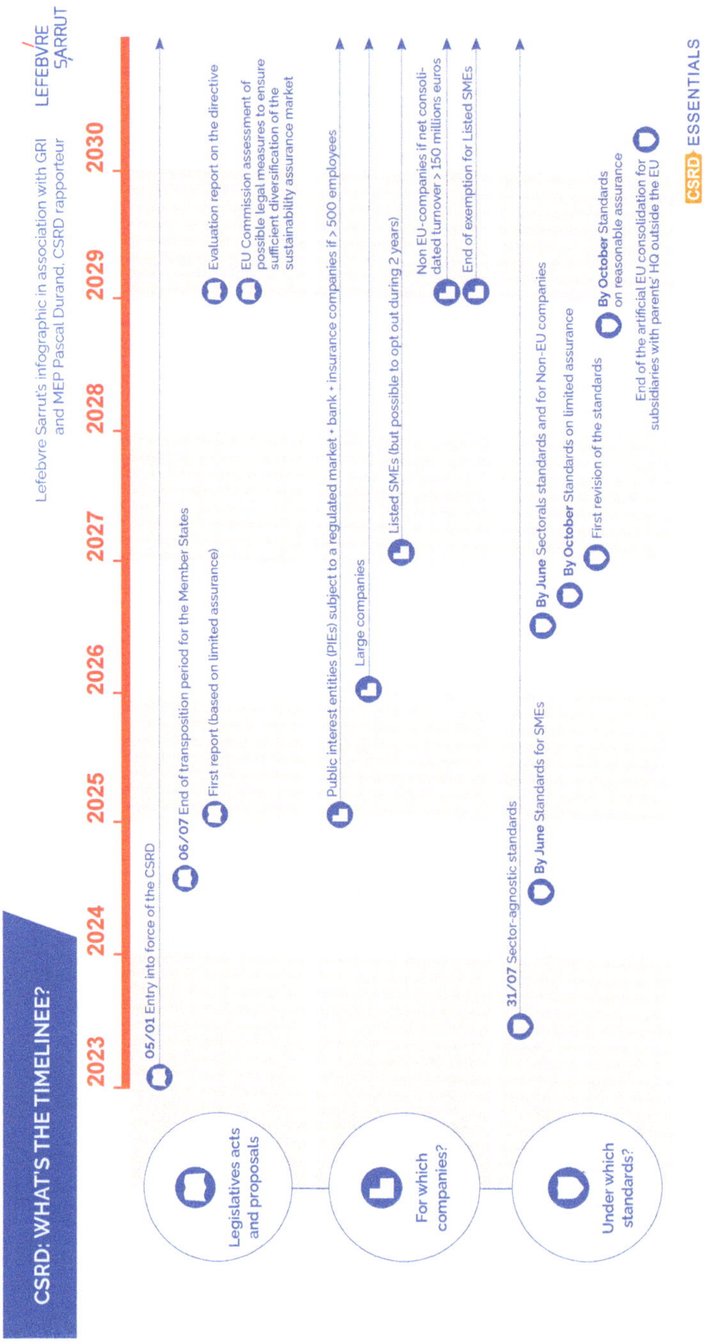

ARTICLE 7
ENTRY INTO FORCE AND APPLICATION

This Directive shall enter into force on the twentieth day following that of its publication in the *Official Journal of the European Union.*

Article 4[225] of this Directive shall apply from 1 January 2024 for financial years starting on or after 1 January 2024.

[225] Of Directive (EU) 2022/2464 which is presented in Part IV of this book called 'Amendments to Regulation (EU) No 537/2014'.

ARTICLE 8
ADDRESSEES

This Directive is addressed to the Member States.

Article 4[226] shall be binding in its entirety and directly applicable in all Member States.

COMMENTS

INDIRECT AND DIRECT EFFECT OF EUROPEAN LAW

European directives and regulations are legal instruments issued by the European Union that set out specific objectives that all Member States are required to achieve and/or implement. Unlike a regulation, which has a direct and immediate legal effect, a directive provides a framework for Member States to develop their own national laws to meet the directive's objectives. In the case of the CSRD, little flexibility has been given to the national level when it comes to implementing the amendments to the Accounting Directive (see Part I of this book).

226 Amendments to Audit Regulation; see pp. 205–209.

LIST OF ADDITIONAL TEXTS

INDEX

GLOSSARY

Adverse impact: an adverse impact refers to a negative or detrimental effect that a particular action, decision, policy or event has on individuals, groups, organisations, or the environment. These impacts include human-rights issues, such as forced and child labour, inadequate workplace health and safety, exploitation of workers, environmental impacts (greenhouse gas emissions, pollution), or biodiversity loss and ecosystem degradation. However, rather than specifying the adverse impact by way of new definitions or criteria, the European Commission has taken the approach of referring to various instruments of conventions and guidelines. The identification of impacts as adverse is usually driven by an analysis carried out by the company on the severity of the impacts, which includes the scale of damage to the environment and of affected or potentially affected individuals, the irremediability and the likelihood of the negative impact on human rights and the environment.

Annual management report: a document that provides a summary of a company's performance, activities challenges and future plans, over the course of a fiscal year.

Assurance (external assurance): the process by which an independent third party assesses and provides assurance on the accuracy, reliability, or compliance of information or processes based on agreed-upon assurance standard. This can include audits, reviews, or certifications conducted by external parties to validate the credibility and trustworthiness of an organisation's activities, reports, or systems. The CSRD requires the sustainability reporting to be audited by a statutory auditor or an Independent Assurance Service Provider (IASP). The required audit corresponds to an assurance service, and it has two levels of engagement: limited or reasonable assurance.

Branch: in EU law, a branch refers to an establishment set up by a company in a Member State, but outside its main place of business. Essentially, it's like a satellite office or facility of a company operating in other country within or outside the EU. Branches allow companies to expand their presence and conduct business in various EU countries while still being part of the same legal entity.

Business model: the undertaking's system of transforming inputs through its activities into outputs and outcomes that aims to fulfil the undertaking's strategic purposes and create value over the short-, medium- and long-term. ESRS use the term 'business model' in the singular, although it is recognised that undertakings may have more than one business model.

Captive insurance companies: a wholly owned subsidiary created to provide insurance to its non-insurance parent company (or companies). Captives are a form of self-insurance.

Circular economy: an economic system in which the value of products, materials and other resources in the economy is maintained for as long as possible, enhancing their efficient use in production and consumption, thereby reducing the environmental impact of their use, minimising waste and the release of hazardous substances at all stages of their life cycle, including through the application of the waste hierarchy.

The European circular economy principles are: usability; reusability; repairability; disassembly; remanufacturing or refurbishment; recycling; recirculation by the biological cycle; other potential optimisation of product and material use.

Double materiality: double materiality has two dimensions: impact materiality and financial materiality. A sustainability matter meets the criterion of double materiality if it is material from the impact perspective or the financial perspective or both.

Due diligence: the concept of environmental and human rights due diligence can be described as the practical steps to help companies identify, prevent, mitigate account for and bring to an end the actual and potential adverse human-rights and environmental impacts. This regards their operations, value chains and other business relationships.

EFRAG: The European Financial Reporting Advisory Group (EFRAG) is a public-private organisation that provides technical expertise and advice to the European Commission on accounting matters, particularly on the development and endorsement of International Financial Reporting Standards (IFRS) and the development of European Sustainability Reporting Standards (ESRS).

European Single Electronic Format (ESEF): the regulatory framework introduced by the European Securities and Markets Authority (ESMA) as part of the European Union's efforts to enhance transparency and accessibility of financial information.

European Single Access Point (ESAP): a single digital point of access to public financial and non-financial information about EU companies and investment products. It will provide for a single digital platform for the centralized collection, storage and access to information already published in accordance with existing European legislation, as well as future European directives and regulations. This includes financial regulations and ESG-related disclosures such as the SFDR and the CSRD. The ESAP platform is expected to be available from Q3 2027 and will be gradually phased in.

Equal treatment: the principle of equal treatment is a general principle of European law which presupposes that comparable situations or parties in comparable situations are treated in the same way. In the context of ESRS S1, the term 'equal treatment' also refers to the principle of non-discrimination, according to which there shall be no direct or indirect discrimination based on any ground such as sex, race, colour, ethnic or social origin, genetic features, language, religion or belief, political or any other opinion, membership of a national minority, property, birth, disability, age or sexual orientation.

Financial materiality: a sustainability matter is material from a financial perspective if it generates risks or opportunities that affect (or could reasonably be expected to affect) the undertaking's financial position, financial performance, cash flows, access to finance or cost of capital over the short, medium or long term.

Impact: the effect the undertaking has or could have on the environment and people, including effects on their human rights, connected with its own operations and upstream and downstream value chain, including through its products and services, as well as through its business relationships. The impacts can be actual or potential, negative or positive, intended or unintended, and reversible or irreversible. They can arise over the short, medium, or long term. Impacts indicate the undertaking's contribution, negative or positive, to sustainable development.

Impact materiality: a sustainability matter is material from an impact perspective when it pertains to the undertaking's material actual or potential, positive or negative impacts on people or the environment over the short, medium and long term. A material sustainability matter from an impact perspective includes impacts connected with the undertaking's own operations and upstream and downstream value chain, including through its products and services, as well as through its business relationships.

Independent Assurance Services Provider (IASP): a firm other than the usual auditors of financial information that is allowed by Member States to audit sustainability information. Depending on the local legal frameworks, IASPs can be sustainability specialists, certification bodies, lawyers, or any other entity that received an accreditation to provide sustainability assurance.

Key intangible resources: non-physical resources which, either alone or in conjunction with other physical or non-physical resources, can generate a positive or negative effect on the value of the company in the short, medium and long term. In practical terms, 'intangible' usually refers to human, intellectual and social capital of a company, such as trademark(s), brand/logo, customer directory, reputation, etc. The CSRD adds a qualification of 'key intangible', which refers to a level of dependency of the company's model to these intangible resources.

Limited assurance: the level of assurance in relation to information that is disclosed based on the ESRS. When auditors provided limited assurance, they are stating that, nothing has come to their attention that indicates the information reviewed is materially misstated. A risk assessment based on limited assurance focuses on the detailed assurance activities on topics or data that have a higher risk of error or omissions, and/or are of significant interest to the user or stakeholder. As the workload for auditors is less for limited assurance than for reasonable assurance, and more reliance is placed on inquiry and analytical procedures, there is an increased risk that errors or omissions in the report may not be discovered.

Materiality: a sustainability matter is material if it meets the definition of impact materiality, financial materiality, or both.

Materiality threshold: in the context of double materiality reporting, it refers to the criteria (quantitative or qualitative) used both internally to the company's operations and externally to broader societal and environmental concerns. Setting a threshold on sustainability matters is therefore necessary to determine which topics are material to the company. It establishes the boundary beyond which sustainability impacts, risks and opportunities are considered material and provide grounds for their inclusion in corporate reporting. In EU law, materiality thresholds shall be determined by the importance for actual negative impacts and the importance and likelihood for potential negative impacts.

Net turnover: it refers to the total revenue generated by a company after deducting certain items, such as sales rebates, value added tax and other taxes directly linked to turnover.

Policy: a set or framework of general objectives and management principles that the undertaking uses for decision-making. A policy implements the undertaking's strategy or management decisions related to a material sustainability matter. Each policy is under the responsibility of defined person(s), specifies its perimeter of application, and includes one or more objectives (linked when applicable to measurable targets). A policy is validated and reviewed following the undertakings' applicable governance rules. A policy is implemented through actions or action plans.

Risks: sustainability-related risks with negative financial effects arising from environmental, social or governance matters that may negatively affect the undertaking's financial position, financial performance, cash flows, access to finance or cost of capital in the short, medium or long term.

Small and non-complex institutions: banks which do not exceed certain thresholds, such as a total asset value of less than EUR 5 billion and/or a low ratio of cross border assets in more than one Member State, and which usually do not receive direct public financial assistance.

Stakeholders: Those who can affect or be affected by the undertaking. There are two main groups of stakeholders:

- affected stakeholders: individuals or groups whose interests are affected or could be affected – positively or negatively – by the undertaking's activities and its direct and indirect business relationships across its value chain; and

- users of sustainability statements: primary users of general purpose financial reporting (existing and potential investors, lenders and other creditors including asset managers, credit institutions, insurance undertakings), as well as other users, including the undertaking's business partners, trade unions and social partners, civil society and non-governmental organisations, governments, analysts and academics.

  Some, but not all, stakeholders may belong to the two groups.

Supply chain: the full range of activities or processes carried out by suppliers upstream from the reporting company, which provide products or services used in the development of the reporting company's own products or services. This includes upstream suppliers with which the reporting company has a direct relationship (often referred to as first-tier supplier), or a business relationship.

Sustainability matters: environmental, social and human rights, and governance factors, including sustainability factors defined in Article 2, point (24), of Regulation (EU) 2019/2088 of the European Parliament and of the Council (environmental, social and employee matters, respect for human rights, anti-corruption and anti-bribery matters).

Sustainability-related impacts: the effect the undertaking has or could have on the environment and people, including effects on their human rights, as a result of the undertaking's activities or business relationships. The impacts can be actual or potential, negative, or positive, short-term, medium-term or long-term, intended or unintended, and reversible or irreversible. Impacts indicate the undertaking's contribution, negative or positive, to sustainable development.

Sustainability reporting: the process of mandatorily or voluntarily reporting information related to sustainability matters, in accordance with the ESRS.

Value chain: the full range of activities, resources and relationships related to the undertaking's business model and the external environment in which it operates.

A value chain encompasses the activities, resources and relationships the undertaking uses and relies on to create its products or services from conception to delivery, consumption and end-of- life. Relevant activities, resources and relationships include:

- those in the undertaking's own operations, such as human resources;
- those along its supply, marketing and distribution channels, such as materials and service sourcing and product and service sale and delivery; and
- the financing, geographical, geopolitical and regulatory environments in which the undertaking operates.

Value chain includes actors upstream and downstream from the undertaking. Actors upstream from the undertaking (e.g. suppliers) provide products or services that are used in the development of the undertaking's products or services. Entities downstream from the undertaking (e.g. distributors, customers) receive products or services from the undertaking.

ESRS use the term 'value chain' in the singular, although it is recognised that undertakings may have multiple value chains.

www.ingramcontent.com/pod-product-compliance
Ingram Content Group UK Ltd.
Pitfield, Milton Keynes, MK11 3LW, UK
UKHW051917100926
8556IPUK00021B/1224

9 781839 705663